Gene Sarazen's
Common Sense Golf Tips

Gene Sarazen's

Common Sense

GOLF TIPS

By

GENE SARAZEN

Twenty-one Illustrations

Published by

Makers of the Pinehurst Golf Ball and
Gene Sarazen Drivers and Brassies

NEW YORK   CHICAGO   SAN FRANCISCO

GENE SARAZEN

CONTENTS

LIST OF ILLUSTRATIONS

INTRODUCTION

A book on GOLF at this time by Gene Sarazen is not only timely but should be of real interest to every man who plays the game. We have had books written by the old masters on Golf all of which were instructive and interesting.

Now comes one by a player who belongs to the school of modern golfers and his viewpoint should be well worth reading. Gene Sarazen today ranks as one of the greatest golfers of all time, not because I think he is, but because this is the opinion of every well known golfer both in the United States and Great Britain.

I am sure Gene's ideas will be enlightening and beneficial to those who would improve their game.

Francis Ouimet

FOREWORD

The man who writes a book today on how to play golf
is in much the same position as a doctor who suggests
a new remedy to an already over-dosed patient. Every
golfing ill to which the devotee falls heir has had its
prescriptions in abundance. Some of these doctors of
golf have been eminent practitioners, from the angle
of brilliant deeds on the links. Some of them, I'm
afraid, have not preached exactly as they have practiced, which is not surprising. Comparatively few
golfers can sit down and correctly analyze their own
strokes. They cannot see themselves as others see them
and they think they do things which they really don't,
or vice versa.

The story is told that one of our most brilliant professional golfers was positive that in his act of swinging,
his head positively did not move in slightest degree
away from a perpendicular line, in other words that it
kept a dead centre from start to finish of the stroke.
Time came when his theory was put to the test, through
the medium of photographs taken in a darkened room,
but with his head encased in a frame of incandescent
lights. He was a much surprised man when the films
disclosed that his head moved inches off its original
centre.

A majority of the books on golf were written before the days when the moving pictures began to delve so thoroughly into the golfing field, and in the light of "movie" developments it may be taken for granted that some of the authors would gladly make some revisions in their literary efforts. Their diagnoses of the golf stroke were taken more as a matter of gospel fact than would be the case today, when the golfer can look on the screen and determine for himself whether the written word measures up to the actual performance. By the same token, the writer on golf today is under more of a handicap than the author of old, for he recognizes that if his analysis and theories are at fault, the slow moving picture will show up the discrepancy and the resultant controversy between the pen and the camera can have only one outcome,—i.e., the camera is "from Missouri."

With this thought in mind, one has temerity, after all, to tackle the subject. Yet there is something in the golfer-author's favor: The camera shows what he does, but it cannot tell why he does certain things certain ways, nor can it depict the mental processes which actuate his decisions on different shots from varying lies. It cannot depict why he favors one style of grip for one golfer and a different style for another; one style of stance for one man and a different style for another. I have my own theories as to a number of points pertaining to this glorious game and the very fact that thousands of golfers have asked my opinion about this or that, and that a great many of my friends have urged me to write a book on the subject, has led me into a situation worse than playing the best-ball of Walter Hagen, Arthur

Havers, Joe Kirkwood, Robert T. Jones, Jr., and a few other world-known stars, viz. writing a book on the game.

After all, however, I can do no more than tackle the project on the same basis that I do a golf match, which is to make up my mind on the first tee that I will play every shot the best I know and let it go at that.

MY EARLY TRAINING

Perhaps I was a trifle lucky, and didn't realize it, when my father, a building contractor, did his best in my younger days to influence me into becoming a carpenter. There is a kinship between hammering a nail and hitting a golf ball. How many times, for example, the carpenter's stroke has been used as an illustration of the correct method of hitting a golf ball, and goodness knows how many writers have mentioned that the carpenter would have a sorry time of it, if, when delivering the hammer blow, his gaze was fixed upon some distant point of the horizon, instead of upon the nail. That does "hit the nail on the head," doesn't it, as regards keeping the eye upon the ball. More will be said upon that point later, for the expression "keep the eye on the ball" is somewhat misleading.

It was fourteen years after I was born in Harrison, N. Y., February 27, 1901, that I began hammering nails, and two years later that I definitely passed up the hammer for the driver, wherein I encountered one of those ill winds that do somebody some good. It was a severe attack of pleurisy that sent me to the hospital, at the age of sixteen, there to have an operation and a bit of advice from the attending physician to stay outdoors as much as possible for a period of rest and recuperation.

15

That was a cheerful message, for long before that I had become a thorough convert to golf. It started when I was eight or nine years old. A group of my young playmates were all keyed up, winters, over a game that was a cross between hockey and golf—the ball, an old tin can, that we batted around the street with hockey sticks. The swing counted even in that game. The following spring the same young cronies urged me to join them in the caddie ranks at the Apawamis Club, which I did, and caddied regularly until I was fourteen. Every opportunity I had I swung a club, and it was a proud moment for me, as well as the birth of an ambition, when Mr. Sparling once told me he thought I had the making of a good golfer.

Back to Apawamis I went from the hospital, and during my seventeenth year practised assiduously. The following year Mr. Sparling gave me an opening as his assistant and one year later I had an opening to go as professional to Fort Wayne, Indiana. From there I went to Titusville and thence to the Highland Country Club of Pittsburgh, to which club I owe a lion's share of my subsequent successes. The point is that the club members and officers took an interest in me as a player, allowed me to do considerable practising and to play a great deal.

It was while in Pittsburgh that I had the great fortune to play a great many rounds with Mr. W. C. Fownes, Jr., the national amateur champion of 1910, a wonderful student of golf, sound in theories and excep-

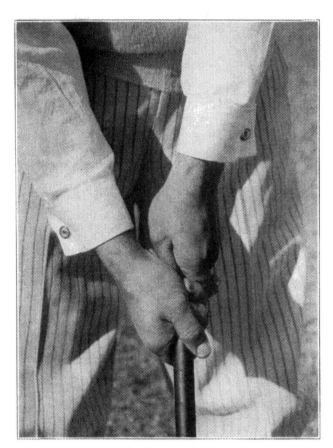

Overlapping Grip

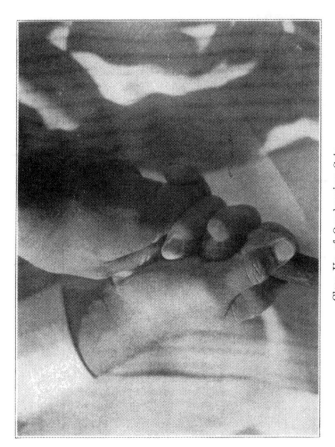

Close Up of Overlapping Grip

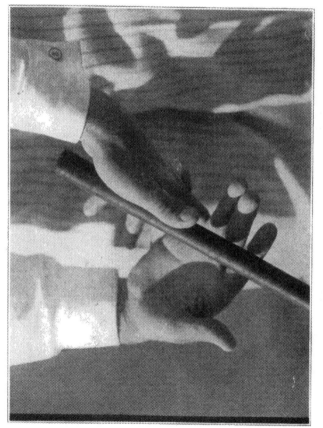

Interlocking Grip

Showing first position of Interlocking Grip used by
Francis Ouimet. Notice that the club falls on palm
of left hand and fingers of right hand.

tionally capable in his execution of what he considered
the best methods. I flnished second to him in a Western
Pennsylvania open and he told me at that time that if
I could improve my putting, nobody could stop me.
From most golfers that could be taken with a grain of
salt, but from him it meant a whole lot, both as an in-
centive and as an inspiration. He took the game seri-
ously and it was the finest possible training for me, a
youngster at the game, to be able to play so often with
a man who was always trying, who knew what he was
doing and how he was doing it and who gave me invaluable suggestions as to where I could improve. These
rounds did much for me in the matter of improving my
play around the greens and any golfer who ever hopes
to amount to a hill of beans as a competitive performer
must of necessity put in hours and hours of practice
on those short shots, the ones which a goodly proportion
of the time will place the ball up near enough for a
fair chance of getting down in one putt.

LEARNING FROM OTHERS

All the books in the world, and instructions from the greatest professionals in the game, won't teach the average man or woman how to play a first-class game of golf unless they be willing to give up a certain amount of time to practice. Too much stress cannot be placed upon that one word "practice," for it is the one thing that will both develop the game and put it upon a foundation of soundness so essential to consistency. There is no end of golfers who have a natural swing, a good eye and who on occasions play brilliantly, but who are extremely erratic. There are others who play much the same order of game day in and day out, whether feeling fit or under the weather. Ten to one these steady golfers are the ones who have given hours and hours to practice and get satisfactory results nine-tenths of the time because they play their shots the same way day in and day out, year in and year out.

But practice in itself will not accomplish much unless it is carried on with some definite object and upon sound lines. A golfer might practice two hours a day, every day in the year and be no further advanced at the end than at the beginning if all this time his stroke was all wrong. He might, through this steady practice, be the surer of hitting the ball, but nothing more. His dis-

18

tance would be no greater and his accuracy unimproved
if his method of delivering the stroke was all wrong
from the start and never changed.

Now how is he to get started upon sound lines? His
home-club professional should be one answer to that
query; the other is, his own powers of observation and
the time he is willing to spend watching topnotch
golfers. One of the finest mediums there has been for
the development of so many crack golfers in the United
States, I firmly believe, is the opportunity which so
many thousands have had of watching players of the
stamp of Walter Hagen, Joe Kirkwood, Jock Hutchison,
Jim Barnes and others of the professional ranks who
have figured so extensively in exhibition matches, aside
from the opportunities of watching them perform in
championships, sectional and national. I think, furthermore, that it has been equally to the benefit of the
steadily improving standards of play that amateurs like
Robert T. Jones, Jr., Charles Evans, Jr., Francis Ouimet
and others have been willing to play in exhibition
matches, frequently against professionals, for they are
sound golfers, brilliant as well, and galleryites who
have watched them in exhibitions, championships or
tournaments of one sort or another cannot fail to have
learned points to their advantage. I haven't the slightest doubt that one of the primary reasons for the
marked supremacy of British golfers over American, up
to within a few years, was that Harry Vardon, James
Braid, J. H. Taylor and Alexander Herd were so con-

stantly giving their exhibitions in the British Isles, enabling amateurs and professionals alike to observe and copy their methods.

On this point I am laying special emphasis because a great deal of my own success on the links I am frank to confess was founded upon what I learned watching others. Walter Hagen's game I have watched and studied, admired and in several particulars have attempted to copy, with modifications here and there adapted to my individual style. When I was partnered with Robert T. Jones, Jr., in the national open at Columbia three years ago I watched him carefully, to pick up pointers from a youth who even then was labelled as a prodigy of golf and a wonderful stylist. I have studied and gleaned pointers from watching Charles Evans, Jr., as I think anybody can who will observe carefully.

And by observing carefully I mean to watch different parts of the stroke in detail, forgetting all about the ball and where it goes. Watch the position of the feet, what they do at the different stages of the swing; watch the grip, the position of the hands on the club, the pivoting of the body, the position of the shoulders, the position of the head and how little it moves during the entire swing.

Any golfer can pick up pointers in this fashion, just as I have, and he will find that for the time that he takes to follow such stars around (so many golfers hate to give up the pleasure of their own play to watch others) there will be full compensation if he can improve his average score by even one or two strokes. By all means do I offer this advice to the youngsters who are breaking into the game. There are a horde of them every year, now that golf has become so popular. A few are destined for the high spots; the many to become mediocre to fairly good golfers. Those who have natural ability, plus the ambition to become top-notchers and the patience to watch the stars and, occasionally, ask them for pointers, will be the ones who stand the best chance of becoming future national or even international champions.

GRIP, STANCE AND SWING

The grip, stance and swing are the first three things that enter into a golf stroke, so they are the subjects that logically come first in the presentation of a few of my ideas of how golf should be played. Both the grip and stance I believe are largely a matter of the individual's preference, though the old V-shaped grip, more after the manner of grasping a baseball bat, probably is more apt to bring erratic results than the interlocking or overlapping. The overlapping, it seems to me, is better adapted than the interlocking to the golfer with short fingers or less powerful grip. I wouldn't advise the interlocking grip for anybody on short shots, believing that the overlapping provides a more delicate sense of touch, while at the same time helping the hands to work in unison. For either the interlocking or overlapping it seems to me advisable that the golfer with small hands place the thumb of the left hand outside the shaft, where for the golfer with the large hands the best results possibly will come through placing the left thumb down the shaft, under the palm of the right hand, although I know of topnotch golfers with large hands who say that even they lose power unless the left thumb is outside.

One of my pet theories is that the grip of the wooden club should be tapered, thick enough at the top so that it comfortably fills the groove of the left hand and creates the feeling of firmness. Then I have the grip tapered down so that the right hand gets more of a finger grip, the club not touching the hollow of the palm. This style of grip for the club to me imparts more firmness and feel of the clubhead. A thick grip for the right hand is apt to develop too much of a baseball stroke.

Many references have been made to me as a long hitter, coupled with which the fact has been mentioned frequently that I do not take a particularly long swing. That carries my thoughts back to the time when I was sixteen years of age, just beginning to show signs of promise and getting an occasional word of friendly advise from my mentor, Mr. Sparling, and now and then from some other kindly disposed instructor.

At that time I had a longer swing, but the way I got it was that in taking the club back, completing the last stages of the back swing, I opened my right hand and allowed the club to slip into the crotch between the thumb and forefinger. My critics told me it was a bad thing to do, so I stopped it, gripped the club more firmly with my right hand, cut down the length of the swing, but consequently increased the tension and got more speed into the clubhead when it came down on the ball.

Both my distance and my accuracy promptly began to improve. It seems to me that one of the chief faults of a great many golfers today is that very thing of too loose a grip with the right hand on the back swing, allowing the club to slip into the thumb-forefinger crotch just as I did and then attempting to tighten the grip of the right hand at the moment of impact. That process undoubtedly makes it easier to get a longer swing, but there is just so much more of an opportunity for a slight deviation of the club-head's direction on the downswing and so much more chance of imperfect timing. On the other hand, I hope no reader will jump to the conclusion that by "firm grip" I mean a sort of death lock on the club. Far from it. There must be a certain amount of wrist flexibility to get in that final snap which adds yards of distance.

There is no fundamental difference between my swing for wood or iron, though with natural variations in the question of how far back to take the club, depending upon the distance called for in the shot. The swing with the iron is a little more upright, principally because the club is shorter, and the stroke is firmer, the driver being more of a sweep than the iron hit. For the brassie shot my recommendation would be a cross between the sweep of the driver and the sharper blow with the iron, except where the call is for a very long brassie when, if the lie is suitable, the swing is a duplicate of that with the driver. The spoon shot is more like that of the iron, especially if the lie is a trifle close or cupped.

As for the stance, there are many adherents both of the square and the open, for wooden shots. The square stance has the two feet practically on the same line, whereas the open stance has the left foot drawn back to the left, in varying degrees. My own stance is moderately open, but probably a majority of golfers prefer the square stance for the wooden shots. Many of them, however, change to the open stance for their irons shots, particularly for the mashie and other short distance clubs, for the reason that distance is then not a chief object, the body pivot is not apt to be so great and with the open stance there probably is a little less tendency to turn the wrists over at the moment of impact. The distance to stand from the ball is governed somewhat by the length of club used and how low the golfer holds his club at the start of his swing. Generally speaking, the clubhead should be within comfortable reaching distance of the ball.

ARMS, LEGS AND ARC

Factors which enter into the golf stroke are so inter-related that it is a difficult matter to divide them into different topics and treat each topic as a thing in itself. Nevertheless, it is obvious that once the player has placed his feet for the stroke, has decided on his grip which to him is most satisfactory and is ready to take his club-head back from the ball, the next thing he wants to know is something about the position of his arms and hands at different parts of the stroke, something about pivoting his body and something about how his feet and legs should perform at the different stages.

Right here I am going to take exception to the spoken and written word of a great many experts in their discussions of the arc of the swing. I believe it was during and after the visit to America of Harry Vardon and Edward Ray in 1913 that a great deal began to be written and discussed about "hitting the ball from the inside," which of course has to do with the arc of the swing. Long before that there had been the oft-repeated formula that the clubhead should follow the same groove coming down on the ball as it took going back. It was when the clubhead deviated from the groove, or arc, that the player's errors crept in, at least that was the general belief.

26

Hitting the ball "from the inside" means that the clubhead comes down to the ball from a point inside an imaginary line paralleling the line of flight. The clubhead is supposed to hit the ball and then pass slightly outward over the line of flight before it turns to the left and comes upward for the completion of the swing.

Under the long established theory that the club travels in exactly the same groove going back and coming down, the clubhead would have to come in toward the player immediately on starting back from the ball if it was to come down "from the inside." For that reason you will find that thousands of golfers start turning their left wrist and thereby turning the clubhead away from the ball, toward the left, at the very instant of starting their backswing. They do this presumably on the theory that if the clubhead is to come down from the inside it must go back that way.

Theoretically, that sounds reasonable. Practically, it doesn't follow the procedure of some of the world's greatest golfers. Slow motion pictures of George Duncan, Arthur Havers, Walter Hagen, Robert T. Jones, Jr., and Charles Evans, Jr., and other stars, show that in their driving, the clubhead goes straight back from the ball, for a matter of upwards of, say, between one and two feet. With Messrs. Hagen, Jones and Evans it is noticeable that their hands are about waist high on the back swing before the wrists begin to turn.

In this connection there always has been a moot question of how the backswing is started; whether the movement starts from the shoulders, the wrists, the right hand or the left. The slow motion picture show that some of the world's greatest golfers start their left wrist back before they do anything else. The club-head naturally comes dragging along, straight back from the ball. This primary action of the left wrist is more pronounced in some of the experts than in others, but the important thing is that it is a common trait, to greater or less degrees, with the world's greatest.

Probably a great many golfers who have a vice-like grip upon their club and whose wrists are like a steel rod from the moment they start their swing, would benefit immeasurably if they would start their swing by letting the left wrist swing back. The whole left arm goes with the same motion and, if the wrists are flexed, the hands will go back perhaps three or four inches before the clubhead starts away from the ball, practically dragging along the ground. The left wrist bends inward and the right wrist outward in this process; and where I think it will benefit the rank and file of golfers is that this method is more or less bound to have their wrists flexible at the start, that it aids to get more wrist action into the stroke when the clubhead is lifted and the backswing completed, up and around.

Readers naturally will appreciate that there can be variations of all methods and that some great golfers can have their individualities which are unorthodox, without seeming to impair the effectiveness of that particular golfer's game. Harrison Johnston of St. Paul, one of the longest hitters in the game, an amateur, has a peculiar habit of lifting his clubhead straight up from

the ball at the moment of starting his backswing; Francis
Ouimet, it seems to me, was a little addicted to that
habit in 1922. So is Chick Evans.

I have even heard of a golfer who had the absolutely
unique method of lifting his clubhead straight up from
the ball until his arms and hands were straight out in
front, about horizontal with his shoulders, the club about
perpendicular, its head high in the air. Not until his
arms and club were in this position did he start to turn
his body. Then, as he pivoted, his right elbow broke and
came in toward his side, his wrists turned and at the
completion of his backswing he had much the same
position as if he had gone about it in the orthodox way.
I am told that he hit the ball very well and was a fairly
steady golfer. That in itself would signify that there
is more or less fallacy in the old contention that the
club has to follow the same groove going back and
coming down. The one factor of greatest value that I
can see in that freakish swing here referred to is that it
surely would prevent a hurried back swing and the tendency to start the downswing before the backswing is
completed, which is so common a fault among the rank
and file of golfers who get just about so far in the game
and stick there, for one thing because they are so erratic.

Getting along to the next step in the swing—and I am
speaking now of the wooden club swing—there comes
the exceedingly important matter of pivoting. To the
supple-bodied youth pivoting is as natural as breathing.
His muscles are pliable, he has no full waistline to
impede his turning and the thing he has most to guard

against is over-pivoting and, as a consequence, over-swinging. The adult golfer may find that it is not the easiest thing in the world to get his body around; but unless he is more than normally powerful in the forearms and hands, and can get pretty fair distance by mere brute strength, he never will amount to much as a golfer.

The chances are, however, that the great majority of golfers who do not pivot sufficiently, or say that they can't, or think that if they do turn their bodies more they won't hit the ball the least bit accurately, fail to take into consideration that the action of the legs and feet form an integral part of the pivot. How many golfers you will see who forget to let their knee turn in toward the ball to aid them in getting the upper part of their body around to the right—and then what happens?

In their determination to get their body around they sway their whole body back from its original position, the left leg straightens out as stiff as a ramrod, they really turn their bodies very little, though they feel as if they had turned it a lot, and then on the downswing they simply sway back into the ball. Ten to one, from this process, they sway forward as they come down on the ball, with the result that the clubhead comes on the ball from the right, and as it is coming in, instead of going out, at the moment of impact, it simply cuts across the ball and results in that bugaboo of all mediocre and inferior golfers,—the slice.

The leg action, therefore, is highly important in the pivot. In taking the stance, it is a good idea to have the knees slightly bent, to avoid stiffness of action. As the clubhead is started back on a straight line from the ball allow the left knee to bend slightly forward, which in the same motion brings the left heel off the ground. As the backswing continues the left knee bends still further, in toward the right and at the top of the swing should be pointing just about at the ball.

By this process the turning of the body, or pivoting, is greatly facilitated, while at the same time the body, perpendicularly speaking, has retained its original position. In other words, if a plumb bob were dropped from the point of each shoulder in the address and again at the finish of the back swing, it would hit about the same position on the ground. At the completion of the backswing the player should be gazing at the ball over the point of the left shoulder.

While the weight of the body in this process comes heaviest on the right leg at the top of the swing, it should not be transferred to such an extent but that there should be a firm pressure on the ground with the left big toe, extending back the right side of the ball of the left foot. With this firmness of pressure on the left foot the danger of over-pivoting and over-swinging is more or less forestalled.

The next danger is that of starting the downswing before the backswing is completed, which is a not uncommon trait. The body gets started back toward its original position while the arms are still trying to go back. The arms, perforce, have no alternative than to follow the body, but they are too late. The body has gone ahead and taken all the zip out of the stroke. The pivoting is all wasted. The body must be kept back of the swing, though not to the point of resisting the arms, which it really backs up.

There is the danger of checking the body at the moment the blow is delivered and if that happens, the arms naturally will be drawn in, which is just the thing they ought not to do. The club-head after it hits the ball should go right on out, across the line of flight. It of course can only get slightly beyond the line of flight before it turns upward and to the left, to complete the swing. The body also turns to the left until finally checked by a firm left leg, to which the bulk of the body's weight has been now transferred.

When I'm hitting my shots well I'm as firm as a rock on my left leg at the finish of the swing, but when I'm not hitting my shots firmly, when I'm a little "groggy" in my play, if that expression conveys any meaning, my left knee is apt to be a trifle bent at the finish. The hit, so to speak, has been just the least bit indecisive.

While I'm on this general subject of the arc of the swing, pivot, et cetera, I would like to digress for a moment and go back to the time about two months prior to the national open championship of 1922, at the Skokie Club in the Chicago District, where I won the national title. I had been slicing terribly and wondered how I was going to remedy the fault. Daytimes I practiced different cures and at night lay in bed thinking

Finish of Drive

Overlapping Grip for My Short Shot

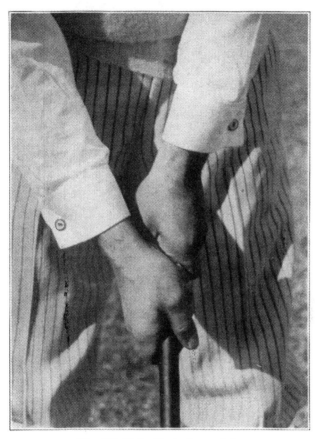

The Old Style St. Andrews Grip

The Drive—Note the top swing, slightly closed—ball
played opposite left foot—also notice that my whole body
stands slightly behind the ball.

about it. I pondered: ''How can I go back in a straight line and come down in a straight line without pulling my arms in?''

Finally, I decided to watch some of the other golfers carefully and try to discover what they were doing that I wasn't. I watched Chick Evans, among others, and said to myself when I first carefully studied his swing, that if he came down the same way he went back he'd slice terribly. But he didn't slice and then as I studied his swing more carefully I discovered that he didn't come down the same line he went back. His clubhead started straight back from the ball, but came down well inside that line and passed out over it, after hitting the ball, which explains what is meant by ''going through the ball.''

What that observation, and its resultant influences upon my game, meant to me can be readily imagined. The basic fault in my swing was cured. Nowadays when I get a little off my drive it generally is the tendency to pull, which is the fault of turning my right hand over too quickly, a fault that can readily creep in when the player is a trifle tired and inclined to press, of which more later.

STRAIGHT LEFT ARM; RIGHT SHOULDER UNDER

Next in the sequence of analyzing the golf stroke and offering suggestion which I hope may prove beneficial to at least some readers, I would stress the importance of the straight left arm and would couple that more or less with the necessity of keeping the right shoulder down. Time was when a majority of the professionals—so I'm told and have read—taught on the theory that the left hand did nine-tenths of the work in the golf swing. Perhaps in the days of the guttie ball it did. I'm not competent to pass judgment upon that point, for it was just about the time that the old guttie was passing out of the world that I came into it. Mere mention of the guttie brings impressively to my mind, if the digression may be pardoned, what an amazing circumstance it is that golfers like Harry Vardon, James Braid, J. H. Taylor and Alexander Herd, all of them world topnotchers in the days of the guttie, should remain so to this day, regardless of the changes in ball, in golf course construction and in the implements for playing the game.

But to get back to the subject of the left arm: It is nonsensical today, I think, to argue that the left hand and arm do all the work, or even the major part of it so far as long hitting is concerned. The distance hitters

34

get in their final and hardest punch with the right hand, wrist, forearm and right shoulder.

Yet—and weigh this carefully—the left arm without any question of doubt is the major factor in guiding the club and seeing to it that when the final punch is delivered, the clubhead's position is exactly right to bring the desired results both in distance and direction. Don't mistake me that the left hand plays no part in the blow that sends the ball on its journey. It works with the right, as it should, the more so when the interlocking or overlapping grip is used. The very nature of those grips is to cause the hands to work in unison. Just as two voices can be heard in unison, however, but with one louder than the other, so can two hands work in unison on the golf stroke and one deliver more than the other.

Where the greatest value of the straight left arm comes is that it prevents the club from straying away from the proper line in going back from the ball and coming down on it. The golfer's body and his left arm, when you stop to think about it, are patterned a great deal after the architect's compass. The pointer of this useful little instrument has a fixed position on the drawing, corresponding to the golfer's fixed position when he takes his stance for the swing. From the compass there extends out an arm which rests upon the drawing at the point where the architect desires to have it, from which he wishes to draw a circle, or part of a circle. That arm bears the same relationship to the compass as the golfer's left arm and club do to the ball. The architect turns the compass, exactly like the pivot-

ing of the human body. If the architect keeps the upright of his compass in its original position, the arm
will go around and around, or back and forth, on the
original line. If the golfer will keep his body in its
original position, except for the turning, he does exactly
the same as the compass with the exception that he cannot be expected to be as mechanically perfect as a compass and he comes down on a line slightly inside of
that of his going up. This comes not through any change
in the position of his left arm, as I view it, but
from the action of his right arm, which is straighter
and more extended at the time he addresses the ball
than when he is coming down to the ball again.

Without the straight left arm it is well nigh impossible to ever become a consistently good golfer, for there
is too much leeway for error. You will see some golfers
who stand as near their ball for the drive as the average
good golfer will for a mashie shot, and in their address
and swing the left arm has as much of a crook at the
elbow as the right arm has at any stage of the orthodox
swing. Some golfers who do this may play some pretty
fair rounds of golf, but if they do, it is only because they
have such a natural eye that instinct alone enables them
to pull their arms in or push them out almost instan-
taneously in order to hit the ball a square blow. Just
think of the leeway they have for errors! They can eas-
ily swing out too far, and catch the ball on the heel, or
pull their club in too far and catch it off the toe; they
have a lot of extra room, so to speak, to hit too soon or hit

too late, to top the ball, smother it or even hit behind it and bounce their clubhead over the ball. I have actually seen that done more than once.

The value of that straight left arm goes even further. If it is straightened out to the full at the moment of impact and is allowed to remain that way until the ball is hit and away, it means that the arms are not being pulled in toward the body at the moment of impact, consequently there is no chance of a slice. I won't say that a ball cannot go off the line to the right even when the left arm is straight, for the clubhead might not be squared to the ball at the instant of delivering the blow. That is a matter the golfer will have to work out for himself. What I mean by the slice is the ball that goes out for some distance and then starts curving rather sharply to the right.

Not only does the straight left arm make it easier to keep the groove of the swing and very materially help to obviate the slice, but it is an invaluable adjunct to accuracy of direction in the medium iron shots, the mashie and the mashie niblicks, where the hands are not supposed to turn over at all at the finish of the stroke, but go straight out after the ball, the knuckles of the left hand and palm of the right hand pointing skyward.

RIGHT SHOULDER UNDER

In coupling the "right shoulder under" with the straight left arm I think I am linking up two fundamentals almost as closely related as family twins. The right shoulder should be kept down, or under, in the delivery of the blow and for more than one reason. By keeping that shoulder under you are bound to get more power into the stroke. If you don't believe it, try this little experiment:

Put the book down, stand up in the position of the golf swing, lock the little finger of your right hand into the forefinger of your left hand and then swing your arms as if for a golf stroke. First swing with the right shoulder kept down and then swing it in a horizontal position. Try it and see if when the shoulder is down you don't get a lot more zip into the swing. Especially notice the difference it makes in the action of the hips. Don't you find that when the shoulder is down and the arms are snapped through, the hips also come through solidly and like a flash, whereas when the right shoulder is about horizontal with the left there not only fails to be the same pep with the arms but there is a noticeable lessening of that hip motion? You have been cautioned time and again about swaying the body and about keeping the body back of the stroke, but that doesn't mean

38

for one instant that the body, primarily the hips, don't figure extensively in extra yardage when the blow is properly hit.

Perhaps the greatest danger in the instructions to keep the right shoulder under and get the shoulder into the stroke is that when a person is inclined to press unduly (there are times when it is perfectly legitimate to press) there is a tendency to drop that right shoulder too far and pound the clubhead into the turf, resulting in a badly schlaffed shot, popping the ball into the air for a short distance.

As against that danger, however, there not only is the advantage of getting more shoulder punch into the stroke, but there is far less of a tendency to pull the arms in toward the body at the moment of hitting and there is far less of a tendency to turn the right hand over too soon, either to develop a sharp hook or to smother the ball. Thousands and thousands of third-rate golfers time and time again foozle their tee shots by smothering the ball and it's ten to one that in a majority of instances the corrective would be merely that of keeping the right shoulder down and having it come under and around for the completion of the swing.

From my own experience I should say that there is a strong tendency, when tired, to neglect this matter of keeping the right shoulder down. It seems as if when you are tired it is harder to get that same right shoulder punch then when you are fresh, and that consequently there is an instinctive attempt to make up the punch of the right shoulder and arm by swinging around

harder with the body, keeping the shoulders in a more
horizontal position. I found myself doing that in the
late stages of my match with James M. Barnes at Pelham
during the Professional Golfers' Championship of 1923.
It was about the hardest-fought, physically and mentally
wearing match I ever played, and at the seventeenth
hole I delivered one of the most atrocious hooked drives
that anybody ever looked at. I was tired, hit for
all I was worth, but hit from that horizontal position
of the shoulders and turned my right hand over far too
quickly. There is only one thing to do, really, when
you are tired, and that is to hit the ball easier than
customary. Perhaps you won't get quite the distance
to which you are accustomed, but you'll go further
than by trying to slug and mistiming, turning the
hands too quickly or falling into some of the other
errors to which that situation leads.

Between the straight left arm, the flexible wrists and
the punch from that right shoulder, come that process
that is expressed as ''throwing the clubhead at the ball.''
This is a vague and much misunderstood expression.
I have heard what you might almost term knock-down-
and-drag-out arguments between leading experts as
regards the point from which the clubhead is ''thrown.''
I have heard one of the country's leading experts say
that the throw comes at the top of the swing and another contradict him flatly, arguing that the ''throw''
is merely that final punch, the final snap of the wrists
that brings the clubhead into the ball with greatest possible velocity.

As between these two explanations, I agree with the latter, although it is surprising how many experts there are who speak of throwing the club from the top of the swing. I can't see but that if they throw it at that stage, they must have their wrists straightened out and most of the force gone before the clubhead gets down to the ball. It is impossible for the eye to follow the hands and the club closely enough to see exactly what happens, although the thing shows up to a surprising degree in the slow motion pictures; but it does seem logical that throwing the club is something like this: The club is taken back and at the finish of the backswing makes what might be called a little loop, which prevents an abrupt break between the backswing and the downswing. Then the hands start down as fast as the golfer can make them go, the club trailing after. The hands are ahead of everything and by the time they get down almost to the point from which they originally started back, the clubhead is still well up in the air, or should be. Then it is the duty of the hands and wrists to help that clubhead catch up with them and go ahead, dragging them along in the process and after them, the body.

SLICE AND PULL

In the preceding chapter I made brief references to the "slice" and the "pull." It's really too bad that the United States Golf Association and the Royal & Ancient cannot find some way of legislating them out of the golfer's life. It doesn't make any difference how sound a man's game is, or how consistent, he is bound to have his streaks of erratic play, where to save his life he cannot hit the ball on a straight line. When such things can happen to the most expert of players, how much more latitude there is for the great rank and file of golfers to strike an errant patch in the longed-for straight and narrow. By the same token, there is the less reason for the rank and file of golfers to feel discouraged when they hit a bad streak in their play. The peculiar thing about this phase of the game is that while the expert as a rule can watch the play of a brother expert and generally tell him, after a few swings, what is causing him to slice or pull, the chances are ten to one that he cannot so readily name the cause of his own fault. It is a matter of common knowledge that Arthur Havers was having a sorry time with his drive a short time prior to the British open championship of 1923, but a short session with one of his brother professionals straightened him out so effectually that his wooden-shot hitting was superb during the open, which he won, and

thus became successor to Walter Hagen as British titil-
ist. We know that Walter Hagen, winner of the British,
American and other titles in large numbers, has been
erratic on his tee shots all through his wonderful career,
but that he somehow has had the faculty for producing
a straight shot when most needed, or of making up with
amazing irons and marvellous putting for the vagaries
of his tee shots. Curiously enough, when Hagen and I
met in the final of the 1923 Professional Golfers' championship at Pelham it was Hagen whose drives were so
uniformly straight down the middle while mine had a
tendency to go astray, particularly in the morning. It
seems to me that after Hagen took to the deeper-faced
wooden clubs his accuracy off the tees improved and
I'm not so sure but that the deep-faced driver might
be of assistance to any golfer who is not bothered about
getting the ball into the air. For those who for some
reason or other find difficulty in getting elevation on
their tee shots I would not so highly recommend the
deep face.

The "slice" is the bane of the average dub's life. Not
so many suffer from the "pull," for the reason that the
stroke which results in a "pull," taken by and large, is
much more of a golf stroke than that which causes the
slice. Moreover, there is in favor of the "pull" the fact
that the ball gets a longer run and thereby gains the
player more distance, which he generally likes. The slice
not only takes the ball off the line, but it kills distance
and usually is produced by one of those hits which give
no feeling of satisfaction. Let a golfer hit the ball "on

the nose,'' as they say, so that it seems as if the clubhead
had gone right through the ball, sending a message back
to the brain which as much as says, ''You caught it that
time, old top,'' and a pull can almost be forgiven.

What happens in the case of the average ''slice'' is
that the golfer has not allowed his clubhead to go
through the ball, but has checked the blow, either by
pulling in his arms or else by falling away from the
ball with his whole body. You, Mr. Reader, doubtless
have seen and played with many a golfer who has had
the physical makeup and physical strength necessary
to hit the ball a very long way, but who has had all of
his natural powers nullified by the tendency to settle
back on his right leg and sway his body backward at
the moment of coming down on the ball, instead of fin-
ishing on his left leg and keeping his weight forward
where it belongs.

One of the common reasons for this style of finish,
weight on the right leg and body drawn backward, bringing the arms with them and thereby cutting across the
ball, is failure to pivot sufficiently. If the golfer will
turn his body as far to the right as he can comfortably
on the backswing, it will be far easier for him to keep
his balance and pivot to the left at the finish of his
swing, thereby keeping his weight forward where it belongs and by the same token it will be far easier for
him to allow the clubhead to go along its natural path,
unchecked, instead of pulling in and coming across the
ball.

Another, and a fairly common cause of the slice, as well as the cause of the ball frequently being hit off the line to the right without being strictly-speaking a slice, is that of allowing the hands to get too far ahead of the club. What I mean is this: We have already stated how the hands go ahead in the down swing and that when they are down almost to the point whence they originally started, the clubhead if still well up in the air, is ready to be snapped through by the wrist action. Now if the hands get too far ahead, and the wrist action does not give a quick enough snap to get that clubhead down to the ball before the hands have gone by it, the consequence is that the clubhead does not get squared to the ball and hits a blow with a touch of the right angle to it, consequently one off the line. Paradoxically, this same sort of stroke is used by the experts in making what they call, or formerly called, the "push shot." In this shot their desire is to have the ball either take a drift to the right at the finish of the flight, or else go straight, but with a low trajectory and with comparatively no run at the finish. Hitting down on the ball, with the hands ahead and the ball "half smothered," gives somewhat the same effect, no doubt, as hitting down with an iron, which causes a backspin. The experts in playing for this shot with the hands ahead are, however, careful not to get their hands so far ahead that they can't get the clubhead squared to the ball at the moment of impact. And with them the stance is different, anyway, than for the drive, in that they are more apt to play the ball off the right foot, the body kept well for-

ward and with less pivoting. It is a dangerous shot for
the average golfer.

The hook is largely a matter of letting the clubhead
get too far ahead of the hands, or of turning the hands
over too quickly or of allowing the right hand to be altogether too much the master of the situation. If the
golfer will see to it that he keeps that left arm straight
until after he has hit the ball he will go a long way
toward straightening out the quick hook that so often
is seen, for if the knuckles of the left hand are kept
skyward long enough they simply won't allow the right
hand to turn over. Keeping the right shoulder under
a little longer also will help in the cure of the hook.

One matter in which I do not agree with some of the
experts who have written about golf is that to get rid
of a pull or a slice, or to secure a pull or slice when
occasion demands it, there should be a change in the
stance. All of us who have seen Joe Kirkwood play his
trick shots know that he can pull and slice from the
one stance, which is all the argument that is necessary
on this particular point.

Obviously, if a golfer has been hitting a straight ball
for some time and suddenly finds himself for no ac-
countable reason either slicing or pulling, it's ten to
one that he hasn't changed his stance. He probably
has developed some hitch in his swing or is making his
hands or arms do something that they haven't been doing. The last thing in the world to attempt as a corrective is to try a new stance. It might for some reason
or other be a temporary cure, but it would be nothing

but a "quack" remedy, after all, and only a question of time before the disease attacks again in truly malignant form.

Perhaps the slicer will find that if he turns the toe of his club in at the time of addressing the ball it will help him to overcome the pull and turn it out to obviate the slice, although it won't do him any good to turn in the toe of the club to avoid a slice and then pull his arms in at the moment of impact to offset the position of the club. Neither will it do him any good to either turn the toe of the club in or out at the start of the backswing and then counteract the effects by straightening the angle of the club out during the process of the swing.

Nothing is more difficult for the average golfer than to play a sidehill lie. There is a situation which causes no end of golfers to change from their natural stance to one that is not natural. But what I ask is, "Why change the stance for one shot?" Much rather, I say, play from the normal stance and make allowances for direction. In standing above the ball, the tendency is to slice. Then why not slice, and allow for it? The problem then is chiefly that of getting the ball up, which is more difficult by far when standing above the ball than when standing below it.

PLAYING FROM POOR LIES

Before we progress from the general topic of wooden club play to that of irons it might be well to pause for a moment and touch on the subject of the selection of the club to play as based upon the character of the lie, as well as upon the distance to be covered. While I am, generally speaking, a firm believer in deep-faced clubs, I can see where a great many golfers will have their difficulties in getting the ball up with a wooden club that has both a deep and a straight face, and especially is this apt to be true of a lie through the fairway that is close or the least bit cuppy. The average golfer doubtless is a little addicted to the habit of trying to play full woods out of lies that would put the most skilful player in the world to a supreme test in digging the ball out and getting the desired distance. The philosophy of many a golfer doubtless is that if he took any but his longest-hitting club he could not hope to make his objective, that a perfect hit might do the trick and that failure would only mean that he would get far enough along to simplify his next shot, so that he would be little or nothing out, anyway. My observations and experiences have convinced me that a lot of golfers would make better scores and get better results if they were not forever trying to accomplish something really beyond their capabilities. If the average golfer has, say,

48

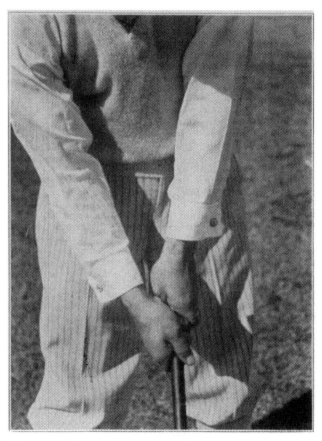

This is the old style St. Andrews Grip used by several star players, Mike Brady, Gilbert Nicholls, Alec Smith and scores of others.

Playing a Spoon Shot, ball in center. Because I cut this
shot more than any other shot in the bag notice left arm
straight with shaft.

Back Swing of Mashie Niblick Shot

Addressing a Brassie Shot. Straight left arm; right shoulder under.

225 yards to go to reach a green and realizes that the
only chance he has of getting there is to get away a
perfect brassie, ten to one he will play it whether he
has a good lie or a poor one. His philosophy that even
if he tops the ball, or otherwise fails to get a perfect
shot, he at least will go far enough to get his next home,
is bad for this reason: That the chances are ten to one
against his getting away the perfect shot; that they are
least even that he will leave himself considerable of a
shot after his foozle, or half foozle, and that if he only
would take a spoon, or an iron, and be reasonably certain of getting a goodly way along toward the green,
he would leave himself an approach so short that his
chances of chipping or pitching up near enough to get
down in one putt would be almost as good as that of laying a long approach putt dead.

My advice, therefore, both as to woods and the longer
irons is that a lot of golfers would improve their scores
if they would employ just a bit more of the safety tactics
in the selection of clubs, and by this I mean resort more
to the use of lofted clubs where the lie offers the strong
possibility of a miss. A brassie can have a little loft to
its face without materially cutting down the distance it
will bring, and time and again a spoon will reap far
better results than either a brassie or a straight-faced
iron. The spoon, when you come right down to cold
facts, is a mighty valuable implement, much more so
than the rank-and-file of golfers will allow, judging from
the infrequency with which they use it. Played much
after the fashion of an iron, sending the head into the

turf with a hit, rather than the sweep of the driver or
the long brassie off a good piece of turf, the spoon is a
great club. I learned a valuable lesson from Jock Hutchison as to the uses of the spoon while we were touring
the country together, so that today when I am the least
bit doubtful on what to use for any shot, from a mashie
iron up to the longest iron, I don't hesitate to resort
to the spoon. The very confidence that it inspires is a
tremendous asset in the success of the effort. Just as
the spoon fits in so nicely for a long shot where the
lie is bad for a brassie and for shots which mean pressing with some iron, so is it also a good idea to play a
more lofted iron where it is a question whether the
straight faced can get at the ball readily in a mean lie.
While I say that the spoon is a great club to use in preference to forcing an iron, I would like to add that as a
general proposition I do not favor either under-clubbing,
and consequently forcing shots, or over-clubbing and
letting up on them. What I do believe in is, so far as
the player can judge his distance and his ability, em-
ploying the club which will reach your objective through
a firm, natural stroke. To force the stroke is to en-
counter the danger of losing the rhythm of the swing,
while to let up on the stroke can result in a multitude
of sins, not the least of which is the danger of wanting
to see where the ball is going before it has started.
That is why so many golfers find themselves hitting the
turf just in back of the ball when they try to play it
''soft.''

Some golfers can get amazingly fine shots cut of seemingly hopeless lies. Hagen is one of them. I quote him considerably because he does so many remarkable feats with the golf ball and club. His strong wrists, his natural eye and his golfing poise all help him to accomplish deeds which are quite beyond the ken of almost all other golfers. His golfing poise, as I call it, is the frame of mind which makes him wellnigh impervious to the bad breaks which are so disturbing to ninety-nine out of every hundred. He is the golfing optimist supreme, always looking on the cheerful side of things; viewing a bad lie from the angle that it might be worse and schooling himself to the idea that it's no use to cry over spilled milk, but try to save every drop in the next pail. Alex Smith, they tell me, could lay a large part of his big successes years back to the same sort of temperament.

These men, and other players of the Hagen type, great out of trouble, did not acquire that proficiency from any Aladdin's Lamp. Any golfer who would attain proficiency in playing out of poor lies will find that the surest road to progress in that art is practice. Now I'm not going to claim any medals for originality in suggesting that for the man who would improve his wooden club play the best method is to practice right off the turf, instead of off a tee. Most any golfer can develop a fair drive, within his individual limitations, by plugging away in practice off a tee, but it is not off the tee that the wooden club play of the great rank and file suffers most, but it is the shots through the fairway, with the brassie. Golfers who on the tee will take an easy, natural swing and get good results, will in a great many instances tighten up and play a stilted, muscle-bound sort of shot with the brassie, all because they're afraid of it. The mere fact that the ball is not sitting up off the turf seems to have a bugbear influence on their nerves. That is why I say that there is nothing like wooden club practice right off the turf and it isn't a bad idea to occasionally pick out a section of turf that is what might be termed pock-marked, that is, an area which has some mean lies. Drop a dozen balls down indiscriminately in such an area and play them from whatever positions they happen to land in. There will be found some real practice in the art of overcoming poor lies and once the player has put in some hard practice following these lines, he will be astounded how easy it will seem to hit the ball off a tee.

Furthermore, along this same line, I think it a good idea to get into the habit of teeing low. Hitting the ball off a low tee means that there will be so much less disparity between the lie on top of the little pile of sand and the lie on the surface of the grass down the fairway. While it is true that the deep-faced club may require a somewhat higher tee than the old-fashioned club, and while it is also true that the expert is apt to vary his tee to suit peculiar conditions, yet on the whole the low tee is a pretty good idea for the golfer who lacks confidence on his fairway shots.

IRONS: THEIR USES AND ABUSES

Once I heard a crackerjack amateur golfer make the remark that if he were teaching golf to a beginner, or learning the game over himself he'd begin with the putter and work up to the driver, as contrasted with the general custom of tackling the drive before anything else. It is easy enough to understand why this is the custom. The beginner, as a rule, is keen to hit the ball. He wants to drive it out of sight and ten to one he has a sneaking feeling that he can. He watches others play the game, sees how simple it is: Nothing to do but stand up and whale a little white object that sits up and waits to be slammed. He just knows that he can paste it forty miles. Like as not he unburdens himself to that effect, and some friend, doubtless with an inward chuckle, some time or other says to him: "Sure you can hit it a mile. Here, take this club and give it a crack." Then Mr. Beginner steps up and with a mighty heave of his shoulders and probably with a backward step with his right foot, to get more leverage, he makes a lunge at the ball. Ten to one he either fails to touch the ball, through drawing his arms up into muscular tenseness, or else he sways back toward the ball just far enough ahead of the descending clubhead to crash into the ground behind the ball. If he doesn't do those things, he doubtless will catch the ball on the heel, or the toe,

53

or pull his arms in at the moment of impact and get a
horrible slice. I am speaking now of nine out of ten
beginners. The tenth may have a natural swing and do
tolerably well. But, the chief point is, what is the mental reaction of those who think it is easy to hit the ball
an awful belt and find it so difficult? Isn't it that they'll
be hanged if they're going to be beaten and humiliated
by any such danged game; they're going to take a couple
of lessons and make somebody sit up and take notice.
And what is the thing they want to do first and learn
quickest? Surely nothing but paste that ball. Human
nature is human nature in golf as in other things. Thousands upon thousands of baseball followers would go
to a League park any and every day in the hope of seeing Babe Ruth knock out a home run, whereas they
would get sick and tired of journeying out to the park
to see him always striving to turn in a scientific bunt.
The desire to hit the ball a long way is inherent and
ambition is never satisfied. The golfer who can hit 235
yards off the tee, under normal conditions, wants to hit
250, the man who can hit 250 wants to go 275; the man
who can only hit 160 never gives up dreaming for and
striving for the 200 mark. Let a duffer go out and hit
a ball further than he ever hit one before, or further
than he thinks he can ever hit another, and nothing can
curb his buoyancy. He may be loquacious about it or he
may hug the thought ecstatically to his inner golfing
soul, but he is proud and happy nevertheless.

Bearing all these thoughts in mind, is it any wonder
that lessons lean more to the wooden club, the funda-

mentals of the full to three-quarters swing, and that it would be difficult if not impossible for the professional to prevail upon many of his pupils that their strongest hope of ever becoming first class golfers would be by starting with the putter and then progressing **through** the various stages from the chip shot up to the full **wood?** Yet when you stop to think about it, we learn to creep before we walk and walk before we can run.

There is undeniably something to be said in favor of tackling the game from the putt and the short approach end, at that. Golfers undoubtedly would learn vastly more about what I have termed the "uses and abuses" of the irons. They would find through progressive steps "upward", as we might say, the individual values of the different irons, and when I say "irons" here, I mean it to be inclusive of everything from the driving iron to the putter.

What, after all, is the big gap between the topnotch golfer and the average golfer? Primarily nothing but the difference in their skill with the irons. Thousands upon thousands of amateurs can hit a ball off the tee as far as the best, and perhaps as consistently straight, but they are lost when it comes to the irons and mashies. Why? Because as nearly as I can see it they won't give the same time to practising their irons as they will their woods; they aren't content to go out with a dozen or two dozen balls and spend an hour or two at a stretch chipping up to the cup from a few yards off the green, playing mashie niblicks from 75 to 100 yards away, playing medium and full mashies, et cetera. No, they want to see the ball travel and feel it on the clubhead.

All these things combine to make the average golfer's iron play a thing of uncertainty. He doesn't feel sure of himself so doesn't feel sure of his shot. He is wondering what club to use and then wondering how hard to hit it. How many times we will hear one golfer query another:

"What should I use here?"

The answer may be:

"Better take a midiron."

Out comes a mashie or some club other than a midiron and if the party first queried remarks, "You can't get home with a mashie," two to one the response goes something like this:

"I know it, but I can't play a midiron for darn. I can get further with this mashie than I can with my midiron."

Now there is use and abuse of irons typically exemplified. Golfers master the use of one club in their bag to the neglect of others and their game suffers accordingly. It is stilted, limited; limited to what they can achieve from the two or three favorite clubs.

That is all wrong. I won't say but that we may be the least bit prone, by and large, to carry an over-plenty of clubs, but when a golfer says that he can go farther with a mashie than he can with a midiron or farther with a midiron than he can with a brassie he is merely admitting that he can get full value out of one club and not out of another. I might modify my statement in one respect, which is that that there are not a few golfers who, according to their tell, do get inordinate distances with their mashies and mashie niblicks, but in a majority of cases the answer is that they are simply turning down the face of their lofted club and converting it into another style of club. A real golfer would not dream of using a niblick for a 150-yard approach, yet by turning the face over and playing as if for a full drive he probably would have no difficulty in making that distance with it. Play the clubs as they are meant to be played, each to do its properly constituted work, and I guess no one will be talking about going further with a mashie than with a midiron.

From the very nature of the iron's construction, i.e., its shorter shaft, the swing is, or should be, a modification of that with wood, varying according to the club used and the distance to be negotiated. The shorter shaft means that you stand nearer to the ball and I might suggest right here that I would not advise more than a three-quarters swing for any iron. The iron is a punch more than a sweep, as has been said before, and wants to be more concentrated, under more complete control for the sake of that accuracy which enables the cracks to land the ball so regularly within a comparatively small radius of their objective when they get within iron distance. The topnotchers occasionally go astray with their woods, have their stretches when they get a little wild and sometimes uncork an awful pull or slice, but it is rare for them to ever get very far astray with an iron, especially anything from a midiron down.

Here may be as good a point as any f r me to give
the lengths of my own clubs, through which it will
become quite apparent why a man necessarily stands
nearer his ball with irons than he does with wood and,
as a consequence, one of the reasons why his swing
naturally is inclined to be more upright:

	Inches
Driver	42
Brassie	42
Spoon	40
Driving Iron	39½
Midiron	39
Mashie Iron	37½
Mashie	37
Niblick	37
Mashie Niblick	36½
Putter	32

Here is found a graduated series of lengths and one
might say the player takes his stance fractionally nearer
to the ball in corresponding ratio to the club which he
is using. There is another and very potent reason why
he should stand nearer the ball with his irons, especially
for his shorter distance shots, which I will attempt to
explain. On his wooden shots he wants distance, hence
he takes a long, sweeping stroke in which there is a pronounced body pivot and in which there is no checking of
arms, hands or body at the finish of the stroke. They go
right through until the clubhead comes right on up

over the left shoulder, so that if the club were allowed
to fly from the hands at the finish, it would fall somewhere behind the player.

Now with the irons, and more especially the medium
irons, certainly the mashies and other short approaching
clubs, all this is changed. Accuracy rather than distance
is now the foremost thought. Where the wrists eventu-
ally turn as the clubhead goes along in the wooden shot,
in the iron they should not turn and if they don't there
is only one place where the clubhead can be at the finish
of the stroke and that is out ahead of the player, along
the line of flight. On medium irons and mashies it
should be the player's object to finish his stroke with
the knuckles of the left hand and palm of the right
turned skyward. On a full shot with a driving iron
or midiron, where the swing is moulded a little more
upon the line of the wooden club than it is for shorter
distances, the tendency for the wrists to turn at the
finish of the stroke will be harder to overcome and the
clubhead will not so readily be kept straight out on
the line of flight. But even with these clubs, used on a
full shot, try to refrain from allowing the clubhead to
come on up and around after the ball has been hit. If
it does, there is bound to be a run on the ball, whereas
the iron's duty is to hit a ball that will not go far after
it alights.

Obviously, the mere fact of standing nearer the ball
than with wood is going to help in this process of keeping the club out ahead and the hands in the above-des-
cribed position at the finish of the stroke, for with a

more vertical stroke the body does not turn as much, the left knee does not bend as much, the left heel does not rise as much, the clubhead keeps on a more direct line going up and coming down, and the mere fact of being nearer the ball makes it just so much easier to let the arms go out straight ahead and be kept there after hitting the ball. In carrying out this process it is all-essential to have not only the left arm straight, but the right out straight also at the finish of the stroke, and an important factor in this connection is that while it is just as essential that the right shoulder be kept under, as with wood, it also is essential that with the iron the right shoulder stay under, as contrasted to the wood process which is under and around.

Hitting the Ball First

Where with the wood the process is a combination of a sweep and a hit, the clubhead being kept almost along the ground for upward of the first two feet of its backward journey and sweeping the ground inches back of the ball as it returns for the hit; the iron, with its more vertical swing, comes down quickly at the ball and hits that object before it touches the turf at all. I have heard the expression that the right way to play an iron is to try to drive the ball down to China and that comes pretty near expressing the idea, for you bang into the ball while the clubhead is still descending, though it hardly needs explaining that the impact between clubhead and ball and clubhead and turf are

very nearly simultaneous. With driving iron and midiron, which are for the longer iron shots, the clubhead
does not go into the turf so far or so viciously as with
the mashie or the mashie niblick, so with these clubs I
would advocate that those who for the drive play the
ball abreast of the left foot that they play the long
irons with the ball about half way between the two
feet, but with the left foot slightly to the left of its
position for wood.

Problems of This Stroke

To become a topnotch golfer one must acquire the
knack of playing what I will call the forcing stroke
with the iron, hitting the ball and starting it away
before the clubhead comes in contact with the turf, for
that is the surest method of securing accuracy of direction together with the art of having the ball stop within
a comparatively small radius of where it comes to earth.
This end can be attained more or less in one other way,
which is that of cutting across the ball, but that is a
dangerous practice, even for the most expert. This
cut shot, made by carrying the club out to the right
of the line of the ball and bringing it down on the ball
from right to left by drawing the arms in at the moment of impact, is employed by some of the experts on
occasions, but chiefly when the shot is a comparatively
short approach and where there is a bunker or embankment to be carried, along with the necessity of stopping
the ball in short order. It is a shot generally played

with a mashie-niblick or a niblick and is best employed
when the ball is resting on a pliant piece of turf, where
it is possible to lay the face of the club well back and
have it pass between turf and ball without going into
the turf but slightly, if at all. This shot is moulded
somewhat after the manner of Joe Kirkwood's trick shot,
where he takes a full swing at the ball, in a soft lie,
yet knifes the clubhead under the ball so neatly and
incisively that the ball pops almost perpendicularly
into the air a few feet and the trick-shot artist catches
it.

Getting back to the aforesaid forcing shot, the one
of hitting the ball first and then the turf, coming right
down on the ball with the more vertical swing, there
are problems to be faced and some that the rank and
file of golfers seem to find difficulty in overcoming.
One of them is that this forcing stroke demands a firm
wrist at the moment of impact. Anyone can readily
understand that without a firm wrist the club is bound
to turn the second it comes in contact with the turf and
if by any chance the blade strikes the turf the least fraction before it hits the ball, and turns, the ball is bound to
go off the line, for that blade has only to be the tiniest
bit off the line to send the ball an appreciable distance
to right or left.

If the wrists are not firm enough to support the pressure which is brought to bear upon them by the swing,
chiefly from the forearms and the shoulders, then much
of the power is taken out of the stroke, for the clubhead
must go on through as it hits the ball to get the full

force of the blade against the ball. Many golfers who get excellent wrist action into their wooden strokes, where the clubhead sweeps right through with nothing to impede it, fail miserably when they try it with the irons and attempt to take turf, and that is one of the reasons why you will find so many golfers playing their irons with exactly the same sweeping stroke that they use for wood, playing the ball well forward and having the clubhead sweep the ground several inches back of the ball, as with wood. Here is a method, however, in which much of the power is gone, for the head of an iron is not the deep and solid block that the head of a wood is and on the sweeping stroke, with a shorter shaft, it is very apt to catch the ball as the head is coming up, which means that all the hitting is done with the lower edge of the club. When the ball is hit with a descending blow of the iron, the descending blade is going so rapidly that its full weight is behind the ball before it gets away, or so it seems to me.

Body Sway; Wrists Ahead

From what I have noticed in many of the medium to poorer players who have attempted to master the secret of playing the irons "right," as I see it, viz., the vertical stroke and hitting the ball first, the things which have retarded the progress most are body sway; allowing the hands to get too far ahead of the club; failure to keep that left arm straight all the way through the stroke and of having both arms go out straight at the finish of the stroke and failure to keep the head as still as possible. I mention keeping the head still in preference to the general expression of keeping the eye on the ball. There are those who will argue that "keeping the eye on the ball" is a lot of "bunk", and they have something of an argument, at that, for you and I have watched no end of quick-actioned professionals and first-class amateurs who look up with startling suddenness after hitting the ball, and yet make perfect hits, and many of us have seen Kirkwood in his act of hitting the ball without looking at it once he has started his back swing. "Keeping the eye on the ball" is just another way of advising to keep the head as still as possible, for when the head moves any appreciable distance out of the minimum orbit that it should hold all through the golf shot it is practically certain to cause a body sway and body sway is a thing that causes troubles galore. Keep that head as nearly as possible in the same space all through the stroke and you will find that if troubled by body swaying you are on the way to a cure. When I say keep the head still I should add that some great golfers have had, and probably still have the little habit of sort of cocking the head over to the left at or near the finish of their back swing, so that they look as if they absolutely could not see the ball with more than their left eye. This eccentricity does them no harm, because the head is maintained in its same position, vertically, and is even less liable to move either backward or forward horizontally. When the head moves and the body sways there is all that extra

Top of Swing with Midiron. Note when playing iron shots position of ball is near center, also note left arm is straight.

Top of Mashie Swing—Ball in the center

Stance for Mashie Niblick Shot. Note the overlapping grip
with this one club. Ball played very much in the center.

Follow Thru with Chip Shot

leeway for its being out of place when the club is brought down to the ball, and from this fault come so many of the topped balls, hitting back of the ball and other common errors.

The wrists play as important a part in the punch with the iron as they do in accelerating the speed of the wood. With the irons they in a way are even more of a factor, so far as distance is concerned, for the more fulsome swing with wood, plus the added length of the club, gives just that much more leverage than can be had with the shorter-shafted iron with its abbreviated swing. Thus, I have known players who could play with wrists rigid all through the stroke and yet get an astonishingly long ball, but in such instances it generally was noticeable that they used clubs with extra long shafts, that they took a full swing, with a consequent long leverage, and that as a rule they were powerful physically.

For the great rank and file there must be wrist action to get distance with an iron without undue pressing and without the full swing that robs the iron of its greatest value, which is absolute control. In getting full value out of the wrists it is essential that their snap be not imparted too soon to be effective, but right here arises one of the chief dangers, which is that the wrists are held back so long that the hands get too far ahead of the clubhead and then when the wrists try to do their allotted task of snapping the head through, the face of the club is facing the ground and never has a chance to get straightened out before the blow is delivered. Thereupon results what is termed the smoth-

ered shot. The ball is jammed between the face of the
club and the ground. It escapes as soon as it can and
goes somewhere on the rebound from the turf, but
either off on a tangent or else for a short distance ahead.
This same kind of a mis-stroke can come not only from
the hands getting too far ahead of the club, but also
from swaying into the shot and,—keep this well in
mind—from failure to keep that right shoulder down.

Watch a number of inferior golfers and when it comes
to playing their irons, where they know that the stroke
should be firm and the body somewhat more rigid all
the way through than with the freer-swinging wood,
and note how many of them in their effort to hit the ball
first, as per teachings, will actually have their right
shoulder higher than their left at the moment of delivering the stroke. They are truly ''coming down on the
ball,'' down on it with everything they have except
their feet, and they might as well step on it so far as
getting anywhere. Keep the right shoulder under, the
left arm straight as a fit and proper guide, hit the ball
first and don't be afraid of spoiling the turf are some
summing-up objurgations in iron play.

MASHIE AND MASHIE-NIBLICK

How many times we all have heard some such remark as, "Jack can hit the ball a mile, but after that he's all done." Nearly every club has its long hitter who off the tee can hold his own in practically any company, and who perhaps is fairly straight with his woods, but who is utterly lost when it comes to the finer art of the middle distance irons and the still more delicate mashie and mashie-niblick. Now I am not ready to agree with those who say that a man who can play his irons and putt is a match for anybody. In these modern days a man who can't drive a reasonably long ball is under considerable of a handicap, for a reason that as the game increases in popularity its ranks are being more and more filled by both amateurs and professionals who are adept in all departments; therefore, no matter how good a man may be with his driving iron, midiron, mashie and putter, he can't in the long run keep pace with the topnotchers unless he can consistently get home in two on the holes reachable by the good hitters on their second shots.

But taken by and large there are, to my way of thinking, a great many more golfers who can hit a good tee shot than there are who can play a first-class mashie shot. This isn't always going to be so, of that I feel sure. There is a tremendous crop of youthful golfers coming along in whose ranks are a surprisingly large number

who are learning how to play their mashies. Many of
them have been caddies. As keen-eyed youngsters they
watch the home professional and the club's foremost
amateurs. Before and after caddie hours they get to
playing among themselves over a couple of improvised
holes not far apart. You sometimes will see six, eight
or ten of the youngsters in a match, frequently in their
prescribed caddie area, where they assemble and wait
for work. They all play from one hole to the other and
then back again. Maybe there is a nickel apiece on the
side; very likely is.

The boys become so adept at this little pitch that it is
nothing unusual for them to hole the mashie shot. They
get to know the feel of the club perfectly and to estimate
their distance remarkably. They learn to play the shot
right. They are the greatest little imitators, some of
them, that you can find anywhere. If you don't believe
it, watch them surreptitiously, some time, and you
doubtless will see one of their number giving an imita-
tion of the club professional, or the club's leading amateur or, more than likely, of the man they have just
caddied for. If their late employer has some oddity,
chances are they will imitate it with a faithfulness truly
astonishing.

You, too, have got to be more or less an imitator and
you've got to learn the art of playing a mashie and
mashie-niblick to become a golfer. Next thing is, what
to learn.

We have already mentioned that as you come down
the line from the wood to the mashie it is natural to

stand a little closer to the ball and to curtail the extent of the backswing. The only occasion that I can conceive for a full swing with the mashie is one where it is necessary to get more and quicker elevation than can be secured through any other club than the mashie, and at the same time get all possible distance. Under that circumstance it is distance and elevation that is sought, more than accuracy; but on all straightaway mashie shots, accuracy is the foremost consideration.

The mashie, as I view its limitations, should never be swung so far back that the hands get higher than the level of the shoulder. The arms should be kept well in toward the body, the right elbow especially so all through the stroke. The club should be gripped firmly, with the hands well on top of the shaft, the forefinger and thumb doing most of the gripping with the right hand. The hands should be well below the waistline in the address. To prevent the right arm from straying away from the side during the swing I have known players to try the procedure of putting a handkerchief under their right armpit and endeavoring to play the shot without having the 'kerchief drop. It is not a half bad idea, for if you will try the experiment yourself you will discover that in the effort to hold the handkerchief in place you will almost play the shot with your right elbow resting on your right hip. Don't forget, however, that the straight left arm still applies.

Because the stance with the mashie is so relatively near to the ball and the swing so vertical, there is little pivoting to be done; consequently, there is only slight bending of the left knee and on medium distance mashie shots the left heel does not come up at all. Many fine players stand with their feet quite close together for the mashie, the weight about evenly distributed except that on the shorter shots it rests more on the right foot all the way through the stroke.

Hitting the Ball First

The mashie shot should be a firm, crisp blow, in which the ball should be struck while the clubhead is still descending and before it touches the turf. Probably there is no phase of the game in which the professional has a more difficult task than in getting the pupil to learn and carry out this point. Hitting the ball first is akin to the draw shot or the masse in billiards. As the lower edge of the mashie or mashie niblick blade comes in contact with the ball and then goes along to the turf, it starts the ball to rotating and that rotation, or spin, means that when the ball comes to earth its forward motion will be checked by that spinning. If there is enough backspin, the ball may stop almost where it alights or even roll backward.

The amount of backspin is governed largely by how high the blade of the mashie or mashie niblick strikes the ball on the descending blow. That is why I liken the stroke to the draw shot or the masse in billiards. The masse in golf would be to have the lower edge of the blade strike the ball as high as its centre. It might possibly be struck the tiniest fraction above the centre

and still be a good shot; but the danger is that the higher
the ball is struck, the more chance there is of "smothering" the ball, or in other words, of jamming it between
the blade of the club and the turf and allowing it no
chance to escape. But for the ordinary backspin shot,
played by hitting the ball below the centre, or even down
almost to the point where ball and turf meet, there is no
danger of "smothering," providing the player allows the
clubhead to go on down "through the ball," so to speak,
thereby allowing the club's laid-back face to provide the
necessary elevation.

After hitting the ball the clubhead is supposed to pass
along to the turf, either to go along the surface and out
along the line of flight, or else into the turf and then up
and out straight, after taking the divot. It will be quite
apparent to anybody that if the clubhead is to pass
through the turf, taking the divot, that the wrists must
be firm at the moment of impact, else it is what might
be called a stab. There are some players who sometimes
get very good results with a stabbed mashie or mashie-
niblick approach, where the clubhead has hit the ball
while descending and has gone so deep into the turf that
even strong wrists won't bring it through. The player
who does that has at least half-learned the correct shot
and is more likely to improve than is the man who somehow can't force himself to believe that the loft of the
face will elevate the ball and that it isn't necessary for
him to get the elevation by attempting to lift the ball
with his arms, or try to scoop it up.

You and I all have seen that golfer. He is almost in the majority. He comes to a hole where the green is on an elevation or where there is a deep bunker guarding the green in front. Instead of coming down boldly and firmly on the ball he tries to lift it, by lifting his club while he is in the act of hitting the ball. About as often as not he plays the shot with a sweeping stroke, instead of a descending blow and with this result, that in trying to lift the ball by lifting his arms, he lifts the clubhead just as he is coming into the ball; the edge of the blade is coming up when it catches the ball about amidship and the result is an ignominious top.

Avoid Swaying

We must admit that hitting the ball first is easier said than done, at least with the rank and file. Golfers innumerable will aver that it isn't the easiest thing to hit the pesky little white object anywhere, let alone to hit it at or a little below the centre, or just about where ball and turf meet. Granting that to be true, there is nothing like trying to do the thing right. The first thing to remember is that the same precept already remarked earlier in the book, about not swaying, must again be strictly adhered to in the mashie play. The danger of swaying ought not to be so great as in the clubs with longer swing, nevertheless swaying on the mashie shot is quite a common fault and more often than otherwise is the cause of that awful disease, shanking the mashie. Swaying also is the frequent cause of getting the body so far ahead that the hands go ahead with it, the club comes along behind and the smothered shot results.

A rather good way, it seems to me, of learning to hit the ball first and hit it while the clubhead is still descending is to select a practice ground, tee the ball up perhaps quarter of an inch, mark the spot where the tee is and then note where the clubhead comes in contact with the turf in front of the ball. The clubhead should not touch the turf until it has passed the point where the ball rested. The expert on a shot of this character, where he was trying to impart heavy backspin, probably would not bring his clubhead in contact with the turf less than at least an inch out beyond the ball. Learning to hit the ball in this way off a low tee, for the sake of the practice and the chance to more conclusively test the shot, the faculty of doing the same thing off the turf would undoubtedly become second nature. The head must be kept as still as possible to bring success on this shot.

Gauging Distance

A golfer needs not only learn how to play the mashie correctly, but must learn his own limitations with the club. Because your partner of the round uses his mashie for a 160-yard approach is no reason why you should use that same club. You might be capable of driving a longer ball than a golfer who can get 150 yards out of his mashie much more readily than you can. You may have far more suppleness of body, better pivoting and far more rhythm in your wooden club play than he has, but he in turn may be far stronger than you in the forearms and wrists and get much more perfect timing into his shorter-swinging mashie punch than you.

One very good way of judging your distance and your
limitations is to start practising chip shots and gradually
increase the distance until you finally discover about the
point where your mashie-niblick gets you home without
undue effort and so on until you have a pretty good idea
of what your full distance is with the mashie. Your
wrists, of course, play their part in these shots, as with
the longer ones, but as you progress in the art you
probably will discover that the application of the wrists
to mashie shots and what we call half irons varies much
more than in wooden shots.

For example, the wrists give their full measure to the
full mashie shot, to help give the distance without over-
swinging. They give service just a little differently than
with wood, in this way, that the second the clubhead
meets the ball their task is to stiffen up and carry the
clubhead through whatever turf is taken, in contrast
to the wooden stroke, where they bend and roll on the
backswing, come back into place on the down stroke and
then bend and turn again as the swing is completed.

Where the wrists play a minor part with the irons,
as the golfer becomes more expert, is that on half irons
and medium mashies he probably will discover that he
can get his best results by keeping the wrists almost
entirely out of the stroke, if not altogether out. Then
this happens: He can hit the ball just as crisp and firm
a stroke for the shorter distance, without bringing his
wrists into play, as he can for the longer distance when
using the wrists. The secret of the iron and mashie

success, as we have said before, is firmness and crispness and there he gets it while killing the distance by keeping the wrists out.

Perhaps you, Mr. Reader (or Mrs.), have been puzzled at times to see an expert get surprising distance with an iron or mashie without any apparent effort and then seemingly hit the ball just as hard to go half as far. Doubtless the explanation is along the line that I have just given. Go out yourself some day, put a ball down and hit it with just a little flick of the wrists, casual like, and I haven't any doubt you will be astonished how far it will go and how hard you have to hit it with stiff wrists to gain the same distance.

I know a chap who got into the golfing doldrums, became so worked up over his poor driving that the moment he stepped on the tee every nerve became tense, every muscle taut and there was no more pliancy to his stroke than if he were a human frame of steel. He lost all idea of body pivot and he swayed like a reed in a gale in his endeavor to kill the ball. On one tee, in this terrible golfing plight, he crashed down six or eight inches back of the ball and the clubhead bounded right over it. Incensed and disgusted, he swung again, without hardly waiting to regain his equilibrium. This time he had no time to think about what he was doing, no time to get his muscles set or do the numerous wrong things that a mediocre golfer can do when he is trying not to. Quite the contrary, his swing now was natural. He pivoted because in his anger he wanted to take the club back as far as possible and whang the ball. His wrists

rolled because he wasn't thinking anything about them
and he didn't check the clubhead at the moment of
impact because all he was thinking about was pasting
the ball, no matter where it went. Result, he hit a ball
about 25 yards longer than when hitting at his best. He
got everything into it, just as does the average golfer
in swinging at daisies or dandelions.

The only material difference between the mashie and
the mashie-niblick shot is that the latter should never
be more than what might be called a half swing and,
for the great majority of golfers, never more than for
75 to 100 yards. You will see golfers taking their deep-
faced mashie, or mashie-niblick, for shots a great sight
longer, but it isn't advisable for most golfers to follow
their example. Many of us, of course, have read (and
perhaps you have seen) the great Ted Ray and his
amazing execution with the niblick, but all I can say
about that is that Ted Ray is Ted Ray. Samson might
have used a niblick for a 400-yard drive in his day.

Right here it might not be amiss for me to say something about golf balls—and this is an important item.
If a golf ball is not properly constructed it will not
carry true or putt accurately. The core of the ball must
be round and centrally placed—in other words the ball
must be balanced. There are a number of good balls on
the market but personally I prefer and play the Wilson
Pinehurst as I have found it in addition to being an
exceptionally long ball to be a balanced ball.

PUTTING

Teaching or learning to putt is very much like trying to catch the greased pig at the fair: You think you've got him and just then he slips away. Some of the finest putters in the world are golfers who find it a tough job to break 90 on the average course; some of the worst putters in the world can consistently break 80. The men who win national and international championships or other big competitive events are the ones who, as a rule, putt most consistently in that particular tourna ment. The greatest, however, have their putting lapses, more so than in any other department of the game. George Duncan, one of the most brilliant golfers of all time, can reach the dizzy heights when on one of his putting streaks, but he never knows when he is about to fall into a three-putt streak. Harry Vardon, the human machine in every department except putting, always kept his followers on tenter hooks when he faced a putt of a yard or less. The curious thing about his putting, however, according to all I have read, was that few golfers have been his equal on getting long approach putts or chip shots up close to the hole, so that he made up considerably in one way what he lost in another. More than that, he and Charles Evans, Jr., had the faculty of so often putting full iron shots and mashies within a 15-foot radius of the cup that they could not

77

well miss going down in two putts, ordinarily, and were bound to occasionally go down in one. Of all the professional golfers I have known, watched or played against, the best and most consistent putter up to the time of this writing has been Walter Hagen.

Now what are the secrets of Hagen's successful putting? Is it a matter of stance? I don't think so. The firmness of his stance, the steadiness of his body, the evenness and unhurriedness of both his backward and forward motion of the putter, with the head going through smoothly after the ball, all enter into his success, no doubt, but I can't see any reason why those things can't all be accomplished with any stance that is comfortable to the golfer. There are a great many good putters who prefer a more upright stance than his, Francis Ouimet for instance. His is more of a pendulum stroke, in which the elbows are out, both arms moving backward and forward like the pendulum of a clock. The main elements of the stroke are the same however, viz.: a smooth motion in which the clubhead goes back and comes forward on a straight line. Where Hagen's stance, with its weight on the left leg, the right acting as a brace, may have some advantage over the upright is that in a wind the body undoubtedly has better support and absence of sway.

One of the commonest faults in putting, doubtless, is that of gripping the club too tightly with the right hand, under stress of competition and turning it as the clubhead comes to the ball, thereby turning the face of the club to the left and sending the ball off the line in that direction. Another common fault is to stab the putt, instead of going through with the aforesaid smooth stroke. A third is to go back too fast and then jerk the club forward. A fourth is to go back to the right of the line of the ball and then cut across it when coming forward. Some golfers cut their putts purposely because they think it has the tendency of imparting a spin which will ''hold'' the cup better, and drop in, if the putt is of the rimming order. It isn't a safe or sound style, to my way of thinking. I have known golfers who in a tight match fall into the habit of carrying their putter head back quite a distance further than normal.

Granted that the golfer schools himself to take his clubhead back slowly upon the line of the putt, bring it back unhurriedly to the ball and then follow through on that same line, which insures that on a level green his ball will go straight toward the hole if he has a true eye, his next problem is the matter of speed; and here is a matter of individual judgment, experience and practice, plus intuition. Experience counts in respect to sizing up the speed of the green. The experienced golfer will size the length and texture of the grass and by walking on the green will feel whether the turf is hard or soft. Where even he will be handicapped is to strike one of those greens where between him and the cup may be one or two soft spots, or where he has to put enough force into the stroke to go over a patch of velvety green before striking a patch around the cup that is trodden down by much play and very slippery, as sometimes happens in a tournament after a rainstorm. Intuition and a good eye for angles count on a rolling green, where it is necessary to allow for a roll.

But after all these things are said, there is still left what in a sense is fully as important as anything that has gone before and that is CONFIDENCE. In the pinch, confidence is just about ninety percent of the putt. The reason why I put the percentage so high is that through confidence the golfer will perform correctly the mechanical parts of the stroke and then confidence is the supreme asset that causes him to hit firmly for the back of the cup, not wondering whether he will hole it, but quite believing that he will, surprised if he doesn't.

What confidence amounts to in putting can best be sized up in this way: You and I have known many an occasion when we have faced a putt of under two feet just a little worried as to whether it would go in. Many times we have been relieved, if we will admit the truth, when our opponent has conceded us one of these little teasers. I don't suppose there is one great golfer who can truthfully say that he never missed a putt of a foot to 18 inches in a match. Yet you and I know that where a hole has been halved, or lost, or a putt conceded we can reach out with our putter from any angle and tap the ball almost unerringly into the cup, and do it more than fifty percent of the time even if we reach out three and four feet, we on one side of the cup and the ball the other.

A world of good can be accomplished in putting through practice, and I don't know of any other way in which proficiency can be attained. Certainly all the instructions in the world won't make a good putter out of anybody. James Braid, so we are told in writings, was a horrible putter until he put in upward of two hours a day for a year or more at that one thing alone. He has won the British open championship five times. Stories come by the wholesale of the hours and hours and hours of putting practice by Mr. Walter J. Travis, whose putter, plus his general steadiness, won him not only the United States amateur championship three times but was the big factor in his winning of the British amateur in 1904.

What is the best distance to practice on? There you sort of have me. The expert who can most consistently hole the putts of ten feet and under can safely be labelled as the man who will win the highest and most honors, other things being equal. For him, then, the logical advice might well be to give most of his attention to the putts from three to ten feet. He ought not miss many under three feet. His proficiency in other departments of the game ought not to leave him too often outside of a 20-foot radius from the cup, for he is playing for the pin, rather than for the green.

The average golfer, who is content merely to get on the green, happy and perhaps a wee bit surprised when he gets up fairly close, will have more occasion to make long approach putts and his success in keeping his score

down to acceptable figures lies in his ability to get his
approach putts "dead", as we term it. In his practice
he must acquire a sort of subconscious knowledge of how
far back to take his clubhead for the distance to be
negotiated. And the further away he is, the more he
must exercise care not to jerk his stroke or allow his
body to sway.

A WORD ON CONCENTRATION

In this wonderful game of golf you will hear a great deal said, and more written, about "concentration." There is no doubt about it that concentration plays its part toward achieving successes, but I'm afraid that we don't all agree on what concentration means. I suppose that to the great rank and file of mediocre golfers, concentration means, first and foremost, to determine to keep the eye on the ball; that it means, secondly, to try to remember to do everything that one has been taught to do in making the stroke. In other words, to remember to go back slowly, to pivot, to keep the body back of the arms on the downward swing, et cetera, et cetera.

Now to my way of thinking all these things play a minor part in concentration. If one is to become a good golfer, these things should be purely mechanical, second nature. When the player steps up to the tee to hit the ball in his round of golf he should not be thinking of how he is going to hit the ball, or wondering whether he will hit it, but should be thinking of where he wants to place it somewhere down the course. His grip, his stance, his swing and all those details of the stroke are the things that he must master in practice, until the time comes when he doesn't have to think of them at all.

83

There are times, I'll admit, when the best of golfers
have some little fault creep into their stroke. Under
the stress and tenseness of an important match there
comes a hurried backswing, or a fatal tightening of the
muscles in the operation of the putter. But these are
faults which cannot be laid at the door of concentration.
You may well imagine that if the carpenter, driving a
nail, tried to think each time of whether he was gripping
the hammer correctly, swinging it back properly and
having each action of his body, hand and arm fit into
the blow, he would have a battered and bruised thumb
most of the time.

We all know the golfer who, after topping a few
drives, vows that he will keep his head down on the
next shot. Perhaps one of his companions had remarked,
"You lifted your head," or perhaps the golfer himself
remarks that such was his trouble. Thus he goes to the
next tee determined to keep his eye on the ball, or, putting it the other way, determined not to lift his head.
Maybe he gets away a good one and he remarks, tri-
umphantly, "I kept my head down that time." If you
watched him closely you doubtless will have noticed that
what he actually did was to keep his head almost im-
movable throughout the swing, whereas in his own mind
he thought his corrective was in keeping his eyes on
the ball.

The proof of this is that many a time a golfer has
vowed that he will keep his head down, and does it;
keeps his eyes on the ball until it is away and continues
looking at the spot where the ball was, but nevertheless

has a very poor drive. The chances are that in his determination to keep his head down, he ducks his head
toward the turf on the downswing, with the result that
his body ducks with it, the right shoulder ducks with the
body and the clubhead comes down to the turf in back of
the ball and takes a sizable divot, while popping the
ball into the air or smothering it. That might be called
concentration, or more properly, over-concentration, on
something which should be purely mechanical.

To me, as I briefly mentioned in a foregoing para-
graph, concentration means the mapping out of a definite object for each thought and then trying to achieve it.
Once I have made up my mind on whether I want to hit
a high ball or a low, whether I want to pull, slice or hit
straight, I figure that my golfing intuitions will take care
of the mechanical end of the stroke, but that my mind
must keep my muscles informed of just what it wants
them to do. If the hole is a dog-leg I figure out all the
possibilities of playing it to best advantage. What "best
advantage" means is governed somewhat by the existing
conditions of the match. There are occasions when I
conclude that the best plan is to go boldly over the
corner of the elbow, feeling that my chances of so doing
are better than ever and that even though I may not
gain any big advantage by taking the chance, insofar as
picking up a stroke, I will impress my opponent in one
of several ways. Perhaps it will be merely the desire
to impress him with my powers of hitting, or with my
accuracy, or it may be that I want to show him that I

fear him so little that I am willing to take a long chance
against him. There can be a tremendous psychological
effect in a match through just one shot.

On every shot that I play I try to attain some definite
object. I size up the lay of the land and the nature of
the hole. My mind makes a mental photograph of the
hole and tells me just about the point that the tee shot
ought to be placed with relation to the second shot.
Then it tells me the worst place for a tee shot to go. My
concentration, thereupon, is to try to get my ball as
near as possible to the point I have fixed upon as most
advantageous, but above all it is to avoid going to, or
near, the spot which my golfing senses have told me
should be avoided by all means.

When it comes to the approaches, my concentration
lies either in centering upon the pin itself or of fixing
upon a certain section of the green, perhaps to be below
the hole for the putt or something of that order. There
are times when even the best of golfers are unwise to go
boldly for the pin, especially in a medal play tournament; instances where the cup has been placed so close
to a deep bunker that the percentage of getting close
enough to go down in one putt is not nearly large enough
to justify taking the chance, as against the safer shot of
avoiding the trouble and feeling pretty sure of getting
down in two putts. This does not mean I am generally
speaking in favor of "safety" play. I will treat of that
subject later.

In my competitive career I never have had a more successful exemplification of what I mean by concentrating upon the task of playing a certain hole a certain way than the home hole of the Pelham Country Club, Pelham Manor, New York, in the Professional Golfers' Association championship in 1923. That hole measures 274 yards, is through a rather narrow lane, with a fairly steep embankment close to the green, sloping away to the left. The absolutely perfect shot, by which I mean the only shot which could conceivably result in a hole-in-one, would be to keep the drive well to the right and have the ball finally take the roll slightly to the left going down on to the green.

But a ball the least mite too much to the right is in danger of holding its course just too far and bringing up in traps that side of the green, whereas in sizing up the hole in practice I decided that the safer and probably in the long run the more successful shot would be to play for the lower side of the green, where there were no traps and where the approach putt was up-grade, with the advantage of being able to hit the approach putt firmly. Choosing the lower side of the green as my objective I would not call "safety" play on a hole measuring 274 yards and I hope the reader will pardon a touch of self-praise—call it conceit, if you will, though I don't think so— when I say that in nine rounds I never once failed to achieve my object.

That was concentration to the full. It combined accuracy and power, no doubt, but those elements I was fortunate to possess in pretty fair degree at that time, yet they would have done me little service in some close and exciting matches had they not been backed by CON-CENTRATION. The power I had as gifts of Nature; the swing I acquired from watching good golfers and receiving valuable advice from some of them; the concentration I had to supply myself, as does every golfer.

Short pitch of fifty yards. Body perfectly rigid, both feet
flat on the ground on back swing, using mashie niblick.

My Stance with Putter

Back Stroke with Putter—Ball opposite left foot

Follow Thru with Putter

HELPFUL HINTS IN GENERAL

The further one delves into the game of golf, the more it is to realize what a multitude of angles it has. It will also be discovered that there are many things which appear contradictory. One golfer might tell you that his most effective backspin shot with the mashie is secured in playing the ball well forward, abreast of the left foot, and then demonstrate the shot successfully. I have already stated that in my opinion the most effective way of playing the same shot, for both power and stop, is to place the ball further back, about midway between the two feet. I haven't any doubt that a slow motion picture, that is, a picture that could be slowed up sufficiently to get a thorough view of the action of the clubhead and of the arms, wrists and hands of the player at the moment of impact and immediately thereafter would disclose that the general character of the stroke was the same in each instance where the result was the same.

What I do think is that the man who plays the shot with the ball well forward has to get his body farther forward in order to have the clubhead come down as sharply on the ball as it should to get a strong bite. If he doesn't have his body forward, it seems to me his task must be more difficult to keep the arms out straight after the clubhead has gone along, unless he has extra-

long arms. You also will see one golfer tee his ball high
to play a high shot, while another may tee high to keep
the ball low. This of course is all a matter of the individual's eye and manner of hitting. It is generally the
expert who tees high to get a low ball, into the wind.
He aims to hit the ball high enough to get what is equivalent almost to a half-top and he is skilful enough to
hit, more often than otherwise, where he aims. The
result is a ball that eats into the wind, with a low trajectory, good carry and a roll at the end. It is nothing
wonderful for the topnotch professional to master such
a shot, for when men become skilful enough to take a
chance on driving a ball off the face of a watch and
wagering that they will not break the crystal, they ought
to be able to hit the ball high or low, at will.

On the Matter of Pressing

You are told not to press. As a general axiom that
may be sound advice, in that the average golfer when
he tries to "kill" the ball only succeeds in flubbing.
Where his fatal error is, that in endeavoring to hit
harder than usual he gets out of the groove of his normal
stroke, generally by swaying. Now the swaying in itself,
is not what does the damage. But the average golfer
sways back, generally with the accompanying tendency
to hurry the swing, and then when he sways forward
it usually results in swaying his body in ahead of the
delivery of the clubhead on the ball.

Ted Ray, the stalwart British professional golfer, is
an example of the man who sways, and who hits every
long shot in a manner suggestive of pressing. Yet care-

ful observance of Ray will disclose that his forward
motion of the body, that half-lurch that seems to carry
him almost off his feet, comes at or a fraction of a second
after the moment of impact. In other words, his body
is in back of the blow, instead of ahead of it. Let the
body get the least fraction ahead in this sway and the
stroke is spoiled.

The topnotch professional can and does, on occasions,
press. Where he sees the possibility of gaining a distinct
advantage by getting a little extra power into the stroke,
and the chance is worth taking, he "goes after it." His
mental speculation, in such a situation, is not whether
he will smother the ball, or sky it, so much as it is
whether he will get the desired direction.

Taken by and large, I think there is a whole lot of
fallacy to this idea of pressing. There are amateurs
innumerable who are so obsessed with the fear of pressing, and its reputed dire results, that they sacrifice
distance to mere smoothness of stroke. The modern
balls have to be hit hard to get the best results, where
distance is desired, and a golfer can learn to hit hard
without trying to turn inside out or throwing himself
off his feet.

Judging Distances

Many golfers have their troubles judging distances.
They are constantly short, or over, and are all at sea
when playing an unfamiliar course. Yet the great professionals go from one course to another in a tour of
the country and either come close to the existing record
or break it. How do they do it? Well, they have more

or less of an intuitive sense for distances, I suppose; experience for another thing, has taught them a great deal in the art of sizing up space on the golf course. But what is still more to the point is that by getting yardage of a hole and knowing their own abilities with the different clubs, they have a pretty accurate line upon the requirements of the moment.

The first-class professional has a pretty definite idea of how far he has driven. He becomes tolerably familiar with the distance of his average good drive, either where the ground is soft or where there is a roll and can tell by the feel of the ball on the clubhead whether he has hit it well or otherwise. That gives him a line upon what he has left in the way of a second shot or an approach.

Many amateurs are steady enough in their driving to have the same knowledge as the professional. But where a large number of them ''fall down'' after the tee shot is that they will not give the time to ascertain, by practice, just about what each iron is good for. They are apt to ponder over what club to use and after they have made their choice they wonder whether they were wise. We all know what happens under such circumstances: The man who, while in the act of playing the shot gets to wondering whether the club is too much for the distance, almost invariably lets up on the shot or does something equally damaging and gets a poor one; or if he gets it into his head that he should have taken a longer-distance club, he tries to put in extra force, sways and spoils the shot.

Of all the faults in golf, no one is more fateful than indecision. Try to learn the value of each club that you use and try to make up your mind definitely before each shot what club you should use, then play it firmly and confidently. Then if you fall short or go over, charge it up to experience and class it merely as an error of judgment, not one of execution. But there is one point that needs emphasizing, and that is the uselessness of trying to ascertain the value of different irons if you play them different ways. What I mean is that it is of little use to turn the face of your mashie over and convert it more into the equivalent of a midiron for a shot of 160 yards, at one hole, and then promptly use it with the face laid back for 140 yards at the next hole. Learn to use the club suited to the distance.

Try to Be Up

As I have watched the average golfer in action, I have been struck with the high percentage of those who fail to get up to the hole on their approaches. There seems to be a wholesome fear of going over. This applies to their midirons, mashies, mashie-niblicks and their approach putts. If I were asked to offer just one piece of advice for a lot of golfers I have known or watched it would be that they start out one season with the determination to pass the pin, rather than short of it, on every possible occasion.

It is the timid, half-hearted sloppy shots which fall five, ten, twenty and thirty yards short of the green which cost the average golfer so many strokes. He is forever struggling to tuck his next up somewhere near the cup, to try to go down in one putt, where if he would adopt the bolder course of banging right for the green, taking his chances of going over, he would often find himself in a position to bang for a 3 instead of struggling for a 4 on a par-4 hole and it would cost him no more strokes to play back from beyond the green than to play up from the short of it.

Why not try this little experiment, Mr. Golfer: In your first dozen rounds after reading this comment, keep tabs on the number of times you are short of the pin, as compared to the number of times you are beyond, and see what you find. Perhaps the mere fact that you have the thought in mind will lead you into the habit of being up. A still better experiment might be to keep the same tabs on some of your golfing companions for a few rounds, without mentioning it to them. If they aren't short far more times than they are over, I apologize for saying so much about it.

With this advice of being up, even though for a while it may take you beyond the green as often as you fall short, there is a reiteration of the advice given earlier in the book to practice often the art of trying to chip up close to the cup, both from points short of the pin and from points beyond. I lay double emphasis upon the importance of this shot for the reason that the man who can go down most frequently in two shots from within a radius of 25 yards of the pin is the man whose scoring in the long run will average consistently low.

Of course, a golfer to become a topnotcher cannot afford to be 25 yards from the pin on many of his tee shots on par-3 holes or his second shots on par-4s. But we all know that there are thousands upon thousands of golfers who find it just about all they can do to get home in two on holes measuring 400 yards, and who find it quite impossible, under normal conditions of turf, to get home in two on holes over 400 yards and up to 450— holes where the crack golfers expect to get home usually with a drive and an iron.

It is on such holes that the accurate short pitch or the chip are invaluable assets. We all know the story of Mr. Walter J. Travis's remarkable golfing career, during which he won the British amateur championship once and the United States national amateur title three times, despite the fact that he was outdriven by no end of his opponents. Perhaps you have not all heard the story, as told to me, how during the national amateur championship of 1908 he was seen early one morning pitching fully half a hundred balls to the green from a point on the seventeenth fairway about where his second shots usually landed on this hole.

The point was that he could not get home in two on this hole, yet he realized that some of his opponents might be able to. He knew, also, that in a tight match it was absolutely essential that he either win or halve this hole. So he practiced and practiced to try to get as many balls as possible near enough to the cup to go down in one putt, for a 4. Mr. Travis early learned the value of that accurate short approach and the accurate putt and it must have made a lot of his opponents sick, to use a figure of speech, to see him halving or winning holes from them when they outdrove him perhaps fifty yards or got up to the green a stroke to the good and then lost it by taking three putts to his one.

Psychology of Golf

Right here, as above exampled, is one of the psychological elements in golf and you may well believe that psychology plays a pretty definite part in the competitive game—the winning of big tournaments and championships, on the one hand, and the winning of club tournaments or friendly matches on the other. Everything is comparative, after all, so that the man who in a private match with a friend comes out on top can have almost equal satisfaction with the man who wins an important title. In other words, if your game is not good enough to make you a title aspirant, you have no ambition to win a title, hence the outcome of a championship tournament interests you only casually unless you have a particular desire that some one contestant shall win, and you are disappointed or pleased according to whether he wins or is beaten.

But you can get up almost as much of a thrill over defeating some keen rival of your own class as the champion can over winning a title and you can have the same psychological shocks, or give them, as holds true of the champion.

"Psychology" in golf is a broad term. You find in many of the written reports of big matches or championships something like this: "The psychological point in the match was when" . . . And then it goes on to tell just what happened that played a big part in sending one man ahead to victory and the other down to defeat. The writers do not always get the true psychological point, for they cannot know the inner workings of a man's mind and what strikes them as being the one particular incident that turns the scales may not be the thing at all. Nevertheless, I will give leading golf writers credit of exercising shrewd judgment in the matter of calling the psychological turn.

"What has all this to do with me and how is it going to improve my game?" I can almost hear the reader saying. Well, just this: Take it from one who, though young, has had a fair amount of experience, there is nothing more beneficial to your game than to learn to take your bad breaks or the other fellow's good breaks in the most philosophical manner possible and not allow yourself to think that one extraordinary shot by the other man can beat you or that the worst possible break against you is going to unsettle you or cause you to let up for one instant in your determination to play every shot for all there is in it.

One could go on indefinitely upon this single point of psychology and cite instances galore of where championships apparently were won or lost, generally speaking, by a single shot. But why bore readers with a lot of past history. My chief point is that what is termed "psychology" embraces a number of elements which are essential to success, one of the most important of which is confidence, but still more important, the faculty of accepting the bad breaks with as much composure as you accept the good ones with satisfaction and never allowing yourself to feel that the cause is lost until you are more holes down in a match than there are left to play.

That is easier said than done, I'll admit. Yet the mental processes of golfers like Walter Hagen, Jerome D. Travers and a few others has been that if their opponents make a great shot, it is not for them to worry about that shot but to make a greater shot themselves and thereby impress upon their opponents that it is no use to try to outdo THEM. You, to get your best results, must try to mould your mind into the right groove at the same time that you are moulding your game.

And here is a pointer to this end: When your ball is in a bad lie, try to think of Francis Ouimet's motto; that anybody ought to be able to make a good shot from a good lie, but the man who can make a good shot from a bad lie has some reason for feeling a bit proud. In the same way, when your ball brings up in a footprint in a bunker, try not to think only of delivering maledictions (mental or verbal) against the man who did not cover up the hole that he made in the sand, but concentrate upon getting the best possible results out of the shot in hand. Take the heavy niblick and whale into the sand with right good will, taking the sand far enough back so that when the club gets through to the ball it will come up underneath it. You will be astonished at what unexpectedly good results you will sometimes get out of a nasty lie in a bunker if you go after the shot in the right kind of spirit.

Avoid Playing Safe

Side-partner to these last few thoughts as above expressed goes the strong advice against playing safe. No matter how long a lead you may have, don't let up, for if you do, and begin to slip, your goose is cooked, or is liable to be. It is the hardest thing in the world to get going again if you once start playing safe, and find yourself being overhauled, but more than that, the minute you begin playing safe you are not playing your own game and you know the old adage about swapping horses in the middle of the stream.

M. J. Brady, I have been told, practically lost the national open championship at Buffalo in 1912 because he tried to play "safe," after attaining a good lead, with the result that he got into one hazard after another that he sought to avoid by adopting the safety tactics. He had the national open at Brae-Burn in 1919 right in his maw, but either through playing safe or else in failing to concentrate upon his own play because of trying to keep tabs on what his nearest rivals were doing, he finally wound up in a tie and then lost the playoff.

I had my little lesson in the 1923 Professional championship at the Pelham Country Club, playing against James M. Barnes. I gained what seemed a commanding lead and sort of involuntarily slopped into that feeling of merely trying to get halves instead of going out to win every hole I could. The first thing I knew, he uncorked a streak of wonderful golf and try as I would, I could not get back into the stride I had been going before I struck this state of mental doldrums. You can bet that when I drove the home green 274 yards, and won it with a 3, and thereby the match, I was as nearly all in, mentally and physically, as ever in my life.

Now, curiously enough, a lot of people undoubtedly think that I was under much more of a strain in the final of that same championship with Hagen, whom I beat at the 38th hole, after having led him 3 up in the late stages only to have the match squared. Actually, however, I never worried much about the outcome of that match at any stage and here the matter of psychology enters in again. I had beaten Hagen in a special match a short time prior to this championship, which gave me bundles of confidence to begin with. Atop of that, I played what really was poor golf against him in the morning round of 18 holes; that is, poor golf in that I was hooking my tee shots and sort of scrambling for my halves. I told a friend in the gallery that if I could go to luncheon only one or two down, with the kind of golf I was playing, I would win in the afternoon, for I was confident of playing much better.

When we finished the morning all-even I was more than content. Then we went out in the afternoon and I gained a lead of 3 up, which he wiped out in the last few holes, so that we, too, faced the home hole all square, and ended it the same way. But this time I was not worried. I had the feeling that no matter where the end came, I would be the victor and you can well believe that is a helpful feeling.

CONCLUSION

Many readers will criticize, I suppose, so much expatiation upon the generalities of golf play, where what they most want to know is how to hit the ball like the topnotchers and control it the same way. My answer would be that as far as the technique of the golf stroke is concerned it is pure bosh to try to lead the golfer into a labyrinth of ideas, whereby he will face the ball with the feeling that that if the middle joint of his third finger is a sixteenth of an inch out of place, or if his hair is not parted in the middle, or if his big toe and his thumb don't simultaneously carry out the telegraphic message from the brain of what they must do at a given part of the stroke, it can't be a success.

What I have tried to set down are the general principles of the stroke, as I think I know them, and as I have analyzed them. Beyond that, I am firmly convinced that the golfers' successes depend fully as much upon getting the best they can out of their native ability as it does to have a perfect, or nearly perfect swing. In other words, you and I both know golfers who aren't much on what we call "form," but they "get there" in competition and we know others who seem to have everything that a good golfer needs in swing and general results, but they somehow don't seem to get the results they should.

Now the reason they don't, as I view it, is that they neglect the little points of not getting up on their approaches, or of being slipshod on their shot chips and pitches, or of failing to acquire the art of laying their approach putts up near the hole, or of hurrying the swing in moments of tense competition or of doing the dozen and one little things that are not the errors of a swing that is fundamentally unsound, but which are just as damaging, in their way, as to have the worst form in the world.

There is no end of golfers who secure their pars on a majority of the holes, and tuck in their occasional birdies, but who for some reason or other do not produce the figures for the round that they should with the general ability that they have. Analyze their scores and you will discover that no matter how good a round they play, generally speaking, there are almost invariably a couple of holes that spoil their card, or else they have too many of the three-putt greens—that bugaboo of many an otherwise capable golfer.

Carrying the analysis a bit further, to the point of querying these golfers who don't score as low as they should, and the chances are you will find that they took a 7 or 8 on a par-4 hole and perhaps a 5 or 6 on a par-3. The probabilities are that they got into the rough and tried to play a full iron where they should have used a mashie-niblick, or got into a bunker and tried for distance instead of being sure of getting out.

The difference between the crack and the average-good golfer is in a considerable degree the difference between the man who wastes few shots in getting out of trouble and the man who piles up the strokes by trying to do too much, or else piles them up through becoming disgusted and banging away at the ball, willy nilly, while in that mood. The topnotch golfer schools himself into making the best of a bad situation and if he does get into trouble that costs him two or three strokes his well-governed mental golfing mind teaches him to forget that hole immediately it is done and concentrate on the hole or holes remaining to be played.

All these points count heavily in a golfer's success. They all count in championships, in open tournaments, in club events and in private matches. Every golfer should realize that there are times when it is worth taking a chance and times when it is far more advantageous to play safe, for even if you get a bad break on one shot you never know when a good break may be coming your way. If you waste two strokes getting out of the rough, through poor judgment on selection of club, it may do you no good to then get out and perhaps hole a full shot immediately afterward, but if you get out in one and then hole the same shot it might win or halve the hole.

Granted that the number of full shots holed, or even short approaches, are few, the fact remains that these come when least expected. One of the reasons why Walter Hagen achieved such a wonderful reputation as a match player was the mental attitude which kept him always trying and never discouraged. I'll never forget a match in Sacramento, Cal., where he and Joe Kirkwood were playing Jock Hutchison and me and at the last hole, 450 yards, he seemingly was out of the picture, with a drive into the rough. But he played one of those amazing and seemingly impossible irons of his, to within an inch or two of the cup—almost a 2 on a hole where one would have gambled almost anything that he could not get a 4.

So, as a final word, always keep trying; don't try to do the impossible, but play every shot for all there is in it, according to your knowledge of your own limitations.

The End

You'll like the WILSON
PINEHURST B A L L.
I've found it to be the
Longest Driving Ball and
in every way best suited
to my game. I play it exclusively.

Gene Sarazen

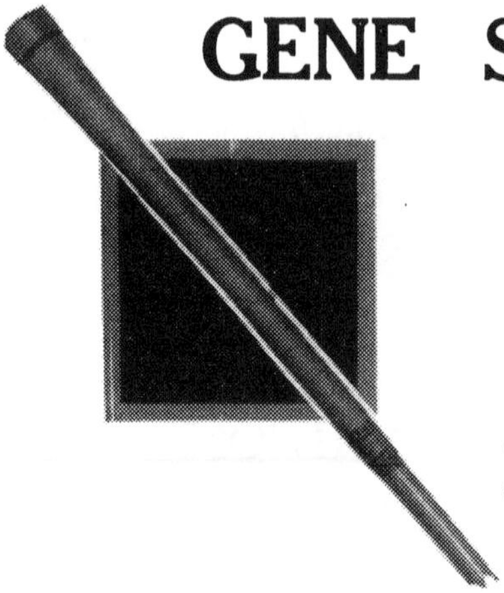

GENE SARAZEN

DRIVERS
BRASSIES
SPOONS

*Made in various lengths
and weights and in rights
and lefts.*

*E*XACT duplicates of the clubs used by Gene Sarazen in all matches. These remarkable clubs possess several exclusive features of design and are considered today as the most popular wood clubs now in use. Each club has just the right "feel" and is perfectly balanced. Manufactured exclusively by THOS. E. WILSON & CO. of the finest materials obtainable.

The

Gene Sarazen

Golf
Bag

An "Indestructo" Model

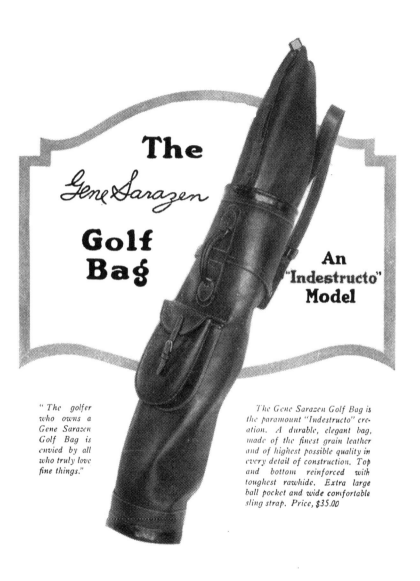

"The golfer who owns a Gene Sarazen Golf Bag is envied by all who truly love fine things."

The Gene Sarazen Golf Bag is the paramount "Indestructo" creation. A durable, elegant bag, made of the finest grain leather and of highest possible quality in every detail of construction. Top and bottom reinforced with toughest rawhide. Extra large ball pocket and wide comfortable sling strap. Price, $35.00

CPSIA information can be obtained
at www.ICGtesting.com
Printed in the USA
BVHW040412011221
622944BV00008B/136